POMERANSKI

POMERANSKI
GERALD JACOBS

Quadrant Books

Republished in 2022 by Quadrant Books
A member of the Memoirs Group
Suite 2, Top Floor, 7 Dyer Street, Cirencester, Gloucestershire, GL7 2PF

Copyright © Gerald Jacobs 2022
Gerald Jacobs has asserted his right under the Copyright Designs and Patents Act 1988 to be identified as the author of this work.

The moral right of the author has been asserted by them in accordance with the Copyright, Designs and Patents Act, 1988
All rights reserved.
No part of this publication may be reproduced, stored in a retrieval system, or transmitted in any form or by any means, without the prior permission in writing of the publisher, nor be otherwise circulated in any form of binding or cover other than that in which it is published and without a similar condition including this condition being imposed on the subsequent purchaser

Reasonable efforts have been made to find the copyright holders of any third party copyright material. An appropriate acknowledgement can be inserted by the publisher in any subsequent printing or edition

A catalogue record for this book is available from the British Library

Pomeranski
Paperback ISBN 978-1-86151-9-962

Printed and bound in Great Britain

Revenge is a kind of wild justice... in taking revenge, a man is but even with his enemy; but in passing it over, he is superior.

FRANCIS BACON, 1625

There are people who do deserve to get hurt.

SAM THE STICK, 1945

Part One

Part One

One

Benny Pomeranski's funeral took place at a burial ground in Essex on a cold November morning in the year 2000, a week after his eighty-first birthday.

A variety of people attended, including some who had known Benny in his and their youth. Most of these latter individuals could be identified by their lived-in faces – faces that indicated a singular kind of past, a chequered hinterland. They greeted each other with nods and barely perceptible facial gestures, their eyes expressionless as they stared at the text of the prayer book: 'If a man lives one year or a thousand, what does it profit him? He shall be as though he had not been.'

The funeral began with a brief introductory service in the cemetery chapel, conducted by a rabbi who delivered a fulsome tribute to the deceased even though he had never met him. Several of those present were embarrassed by this. Or it made them laugh. Especially when the rabbi referred to 'Benjamin' as 'a highly respectable businessman'.

Benny's son Simon recited the mourner's prayer – the Kaddish – pleading for 'abundant peace from heaven' and glorifying the not-to-be-spoken name of the 'Holy One' who is 'beyond all the blessings... that are ever spoken in the world'. And then Simon Pomeranski and his mother, Bertha, led the congregation to the open grave where the late Benjamin Immanuel Pomeranski –

otherwise known as Benny the Fixer – lay inside his sealed-in coffin.

Most of the men in the throng around the grave took a turn at thrusting one of two shovels, placed there for the purpose, into a pile of clay-laden earth at the edge of the plot and emptying a clump or two of it over what Benny would have called his 'wooden overcoat' before passing the shovel on to the next man. As this all-male ritual proceeded, the accumulating soil sliding across the coffin's surface like a brush caressing a drum, one or two of the women cried, though not Bertha.

Once the last man had released the last shovelful of soil, and Simon had been called upon by the rabbi to repeat the Kaddish, two gravediggers stepped forward from the sidelines, each taking hold of one of the shovels with which to consummate the earthly existence of Benny Pomeranski. The mourners, meanwhile, made their way back to the chapel, once again with Bertha and Simon Pomeranski at the head but this time closely followed by Simon's wife, Marina, and their two sons, Will and Jonathan.

As they neared the open doors of the chapel, Simon looked around him with curiosity and whispered to his mother, 'I'm amazed to see all these people. I didn't expect anybody from the Astorian days to show up. They do seem familiar, a lot of them, but I can't actually place them. Except for Spanish Joe, of course. Look at him. He's hardly changed. If he dyed his grey hair black, he'd look exactly as he did forty-odd years ago strolling through Excelsior Arcade. I thought he went to live abroad.'

'He ran away,' Bertha said tersely. And then, in a more acquiescent tone: 'But it is good to see him here. It's right that he should be here...'

'Just a minute... right at the back. Look.' Simon was suddenly excited. 'Can you see? That woman, the one dressed all in black.

Isn't that Aunty Estelle? God knows how many years it's been since I last saw her – or heard her singing on the radio.'

Before Bertha could answer, a large man with unkempt, bushy eyebrows shuffled towards her. 'Hullo, Berth. Sorry to hear about old Benny passing,' he said, curling down his already stooping posture to give Bertha a quick hug and utter the traditional condolatory wish for a principal mourner to enjoy a 'long life'. Turning his ragged eyebrows towards Simon, the stranger extended a bear-paw hand, his blank expression giving way to a smile.

'I wish you long life, sunshine,' he said, squeezing Simon's fingers in an unexpectedly strong handshake. 'Bet you don't remember me. Harry. Fancy Goods Harry.' And, no, Benny and Bertha's only child did not at that moment recognise this gravel-voiced stranger who held him in the grip of strong, hairy-knuckled fingers. But the fact that 'Fancy Goods' Harry felt the need to identify himself by that curious epithet brought a knowing smile to Simon Pomeranski's face.

'Of course I remember you,' he lied.

In the last, failing days of his father's illness, the inner eye of Simon Pomeranski's imagination had increasingly presented images of his childhood, many of them reminding him of what he, as a boy, had regarded as the glamorous and exciting life led by Benny and his colourful, rule-breaking friends and associates with their obligatory nicknames. Benny's moniker, 'Fixer' – or sometimes the Yiddish term, *Macher* – fitted him well, as not only could he fix most of the day-to-day problems within his locally limited sphere, but he also possessed natural leadership qualities. If anybody asked him about his sobriquet, Benny the Fixer/Macher would say, 'It's because I'm decisive.'

Several of Simon's recollections and flashbacks during this period were triggered by music. An especially vivid memory emerged out of the blue one evening as he was driving past his parents' flat in Highgate, North London, less than a month before his father's death. This was a frequent route home for Simon from the drama school in Blackheath, South London, where he taught. It was a long drive, often through slow traffic, and sometimes he would stop for 'a cup of tea and a digestive' with Bertha and Benny. But, though it had been an exceptionally demanding day, this was not one of those occasions.

As he drew level with the building in which his parents lived, he slowed down, halted and then inched his car forward while considering whether he could, after all, summon up the effort to call in on Bertha and Benny. He stopped the car again, flush with the kerb, braked and pressed a button on his car radio, which produced a faintly familiar woodwind theme alongside what sounded like a piano imitating muffled sleigh bells. Suddenly, Simon Pomeranski was startled out of his indecision by the voice of the singer Doris Day blowing through the car like a current of air from the 1950s:

> *Once I had a secret love*
> *That lived within the heart of me...*

Simon was instantaneously transported back to a long-forgotten moment at the former Pomeranski family house south of the river in Brixton. It was his parents' tenth wedding anniversary celebrations in 1954. Relatives and other guests had just drunk a toast and given three cheers to Bertha and Benny. And then Benny had ostentatiously held up his arms and called for silence as Aunty Estelle, so pretty and mysterious, stood up in the centre of the Pomeranskis' large living room and sung the words that, over four decades later, were coming out of the radio in Simon's *shprauncy* BMW:

All too soon my secret love
Became impatient to be free.

To the best of his knowledge, Simon hadn't heard the song since he was eight years old and enraptured by the woman singing at his parents' party. Now, as he leaned back in the seat of his car listening to the radio, the engine's rhythmic sound accompanying the voice of the famous American singer, he unexpectedly caught sight of Benny in the rear-view mirror. He was walking the last few steps to his home, unsteady and bent against an unforgiving wind, trying without success to pat down an insistently floating strand of dust-grey hair. Simon did not call out or drive back, and Benny had no idea that he was being watched.

Until then, Simon had never noticed any obviously damning marks of age upon his father. But now, it seemed, this was no longer Benny the Fixer, the Macher, who his son was gazing at in the reflection. No, this was the old and fading Benjamin Immanuel Pomeranski – a name hitherto brought out and dusted only on high days, holy days, or for the odd court appearance, and which, a few months after the Fixer's burial, would be engraved on his tombstone.

Simon Pomeranski sighed heavily, released the handbrake and drove away as his father turned the key to take him into the small apartment block in which his and Bertha's flat was situated. And Doris Day faded into the night:

And my secret love's no secret any more

Unlike Bertha, Estelle had certainly been at least loosely connected to that Brixton crew of which Fancy Goods Harry had been a member – the Astorians, as they called themselves. Bertha, who often referred to them as 'overgrown schoolchildren', mostly remained aloof from their doings.

Could that woman at the funeral, standing apart from the main cluster of mourners, really be Estelle, the bewitching creature Simon remembered from his childhood? When she finally caught up with the rest of the funeral guests gathered outside the prayer house, he assumed he'd been mistaken. For, beneath the expensive-looking black hat, and inside the expensive-looking black coat, stood a frail, nervous woman, with trembling hands and thinning hair framing a deeply lined, sallow face. Surely this couldn't be her?

But when she greeted the bereaved mother and son with a smile of resigned sadness, Bertha visibly stiffened and the black-coated old lady silently mouthed to Simon the word 'Estelle' before patting his cheek, as though he was still a child rather than a man in his fifties, and walking slowly away.

A few minutes into the journey home, alone with her son in the back seat of the undertaker's limousine, her daughter-in-law and grandsons having gone ahead, Bertha broke the silence: 'Estelle was there,' she said, looking straight in front of her and not at Simon, 'because – well, for a start, she wasn't your aunt. Or anybody's aunt, for that matter. Not really. Not by blood. She used to bring you presents when you were a kid and you called her "Aunty" because, well, I suppose that's how we would have introduced her to you. Every adult was an "aunty" or an "uncle" in those days, whether or not they were family.'

Bertha's voice was strained but firm as she went on to deliver a surprisingly eloquent monologue telling her son about his father's long love affair with Estelle Davis.

Simon knew that Estelle had a daughter, Gloria, one year younger than he was, the child of Estelle's former husband – 'a drunk, like Estelle' according to Bertha – not only because Gloria had achieved a degree of fame as a performer on the American stage but also because she had briefly been a student of his in his early days as a drama teacher decades earlier. He recalled her leaving after a handful of lessons to try her hand at acting school in New York, where her father was then working as a doorman at a hotel.

But Estelle, Bertha revealed quietly in the back of the hearse, had also had an abortion. 'It was a "secret" abortion,' Bertha said. 'Some secret! Just about everybody in Brixton knew about it, and they also knew that it had almost certainly been instigated – and doubtless paid for – by your father.' Then, before concluding this illuminating conversation, Bertha imparted a strange admiration for her late husband's mistress: 'She had a lovely singing voice and was very beautiful when she was younger.'

Two

'Listen, darling, you let me down in there tonight.' Norris Blackstone, the American promoter who had negotiated what he called a 'fantabulous' deal for Estelle Davis to sing at the White Parrot club in Kingston, Jamaica, was now sitting alongside her on a sofa in his room at the Champagne Court Hotel – of which the White Parrot Club formed a part – expressing his discontent. He had summoned her immediately after the expiry of the thin ripple of applause that followed the closing song of Estelle's first Jamaican night, in the month of February 1955.

She was still sheathed in the silky white dress Benny Pomeranski had provided for her debut. She felt a little uneasy wearing it outside the club environment but Blackstone had sent for her the moment the show closed so she'd had no time to change.

'You were drinking in between numbers,' the promoter said. 'I can't have my girls boozing. Really, I should cut your pay, but…' Blackstone paused, smiled a sickly smile, took in a breath and then expelled it… 'at least you look the part in that dress.' And, smiling again, he placed his hand at the point where the silvery whiteness of the material divided to expose her thighs.

Her singing might have been a bit off earlier, he told her – 'below par, if you know what I mean' – but, he suggested, moving his hand a little further along her leg, she could make it up to him then and there in that hotel room. And, just to prove he was a reasonable man and to show her there were no hard feelings, Norris Blackstone offered to give her some *extra* cash, even though, he reminded her, she didn't deserve it. And, to confirm what a kind and sympathetic fellow he was, he put his arm around her. And showed his affection by pushing his tongue between her lips.

She knew she had been far from her best in that nervous first performance at the imposing White Parrot, the climax of an exciting assignment singing to wealthy customers on a Caribbean cruise ship. It was the most exotic venue she had ever seen. This was her big chance, and she found it a little intimidating. She had downed a couple of rums just to steady her nerves. And, though a lack of familiarity with some of the songs she had been given to sing produced a slight hesitancy, she still felt she had held the White Parrot audience's attention – on account of that sublime dress if nothing else. It was a shame that Benny couldn't have been there to see her in it, singing in such smart surroundings before a sizeable and sophisticated crowd of people. The dress, thanks to him, gave Estelle a feeling of superiority, of keep-your-hands-off sexual independence, of confidence – seriously reinforced by the package in the 'secret pocket' of her capacious evening bag.

In return for Benny giving her a dress worth 'nearly a hundred pounds' for her 'once-in-a-lifetime' booking in the Caribbean, she had agreed, with a readiness that surprised even her, to a dangerous request. She was to deliver to a Mr Jeffrey Calloway – a local Kingston cloth merchant with whom Benny did business – a compact J-frame Smith & Wesson revolver for him to 'scare off' some local hoodlum who'd been giving him a bit of trouble. She was due to meet Calloway that night in the foyer of the very hotel – the Champagne Court – where, in a fourth-floor suite, she was at that moment being both berated and fondled by a slick-haired, self-styled 'impresario'.

Estelle took hold of Blackstone's wrist and, in one movement, flung his hand away from her and stood up. She quickly grabbed her bag – a sequinned one to go with the dress – from where she had put it down on a table by the door and went to leave the room. But the American laughed and stood between Estelle and the door. He was still laughing as Estelle reached into her bag and produced the Smith & Wesson.

She knew that Calloway was waiting for her, and the gun, downstairs in the hotel lobby. She also knew him to be a hard-hitting character who would surely take her part against the creep now tentatively moving towards her, his face white with terror. 'Back off,' she yelled at Blackstone, waving the gun, which was feeling lighter by the second.

'Look, I didn't mean anything,' he said. 'I was only being friendly. Wanting to make it up after the disappointing show. I know that you can do so much better. You're normally such a great singer.' And, taking a slow half-step forward, he yelled: 'I offered you more money!'

'Shut up,' she told him, indicating with the gun that he should keep his distance. She was feeling completely secure now and calmly picked up the phone, told the sing-song girly voice on reception her name and that she was meeting a Mr Jeffrey Calloway: 'I am ready to see him in room number forty-six, so could you send him up, please?'

When Jeffrey Calloway knocked, Estelle called for him to come in and his eyes quickly took in the scene. 'What's going on,' he asked angrily. The question was directed at Estelle: 'What are you doing with that shooter?'

'This worm was trying it on. It seems if I want to get paid, I gotta let blokes rape me.'

'That's not how it was, Mister.' The immobilised American promoter had never felt fear like this. On the one side, as he saw it, there was a deranged floosie songbird with a Smith & Wesson getting hot in her hand and, on the other, was her big, bad and furious associate, who may even have been her boyfriend for all this poor sap knew.

Norris Blackstone looked pleadingly at the tough-looking young character who had intruded into his room. In the American's frenzied mind, the conspicuously well-dressed Mr Calloway was almost certainly something to do with whatever criminal set-up there was in 1950s Kingston and would want something from him – or injure or even kill him.

'Honest, I swear it. She's got the wrong end of the stick,' Blackstone screeched. And continued at an increasingly rapid rate: 'Something's not right with her tonight. Usually such a great singer. She's one of my performers from the cruise ship. The best. But she fluffed her numbers in the club. I am responsible to the customers. You must understand. I was just trying to find out what was the matter. Cheer her up a little – you know. That's all. I would never rape anyone.'

'Get out of here,' Calloway yelled. 'And keep your mouth shut.'

'But this is my room,' the hapless promoter feebly protested.

Calloway shot a quizzical glance at Estelle, and she began to laugh, though still standing firm, legs apart, grip steady on the S&W. 'Yes,' she said, and struggled to get the further words out through her mounting laughter, 'it is his room.'

'Okay,' said Jeff Calloway to Blackstone, whose pale-blue ruffled evening shirt was by now soaked in sweat. 'We'll leave but you come with us.' Then Calloway turned to Estelle, nodded his head at the revolver and said: 'For God's sake, put that thing away.'

As the three of them made their way down to the hotel lobby, Jeff Calloway told the American chancer that he and Miss Davis were about to have a quiet drink on the terrace and that they did not want to be disturbed, whether it be by the local police chief who, said Calloway, was 'a personal friend of mine'. Or the hotel manager – 'another friend of mine' – or anybody else. The reduced 'impresario' was told to keep his 'trap' shut – 'you didn't see any gun' – and to keep his personal distance because, the sharp-suited Mister Calloway added: 'If you give Miss Davis any more trouble of any kind, even when you're back on the ship, where I also have connections, I am going to see to it personally that you lose all of your teeth, and that's the minimum.'

Once Norris Blackstone had scampered away and Jeff Calloway and Estelle Davis were alone on the shaded hotel terrace drinking Bacardis, Estelle lit a cigarette and opened her evening bag just enough for Jeff to make out the contents. Grinning, she said, 'Benny says you might need this.'

Jeff hissed his anger at Estelle. 'Why on earth did you let that feller see the weapon?'

'I told you. He was going to rape me.'

'Well, look, I don't want it now. I want nothing to do with it. I'm not touching it. You can take it back,' said Jeff.

'Take it back? You must be joking,' Estelle retorted. 'Do you realise the risks I've taken bringing this out here,' as she tapped her evening bag, 'and I don't want to take it back. You wouldn't be very popular if I told Benny you made me take it back.'

After a pause, Jeff dropped his voice to a whisper and replied, 'Okay, look, let's not talk too loud. Let's just finish our drinks and go to my car. You can pass it to me there. And please be discreet.'

Jeff Calloway had already decided, in the wake of the hotel-room encounter with Norris Blackstone, to abandon his intention to use the weapon for a spot of redress, and the only part of his original plan that he now intended to carry out was the last part – dumping the gun in the sea from a boat well offshore.

When he told Estelle this, she drew on her cigarette, exhaled, sucked in her lips, hesitated, and then reached into her bag and caressed the cold metal of the Smith & Wesson in the 'secret pocket'. She took a deep breath, screwed her cigarette into an ashtray, started to stand up, sat down again and said: 'Chucking it into the sea? That would be a shame. A waste. Okay. I'll take it back to the boys in Brixton.'

'Or maybe keep it for protection,' she added softly to herself, still relishing the feeling that she had experienced while holding the gun in her hand in the Champagne Court Hotel's room forty-six. 'Or,' she whispered a little louder, 'getting even.'

A week later, when she was back performing on the ship during its return journey to Southampton, she exchanged the barest few words possible with Norris Blackstone who, for his part, avoided her as much as he could. And if they happened to pass or find themselves seated near each other, she would treat him to a condescending smile augmented in the evenings by a gentle patting of her sequinned bag, her smirk discernible from any angle.

By her actions and expressions, she would make sure that Norris Blackstone always treated her with respect – and a little fear. Her singing, contained in a slightly smaller number of evening performances than on the outward journey, certainly drew respect. Glowing in the warmth of consistent, enthusiastic applause, spotlighted in luminous contrast with the Atlantic night skies, she unwaveringly delivered the goods. And, though she drank more booze than she could afford, she held on to the incomparable feeling of power that had flowed through her in the Champagne Court.

She couldn't wait to get back to London and tell her friend Ruth how good revenge felt and how easy it was – 'with a gun in your bag'.

Three

Benny Pomeranski was born shortly after the First World War into a frugally furnished but overcrowded flat in a dilapidated building in Bethnal Green in the East End of London. His parents, Alf (born Abraham) and Hetty (Hadassah), were impoverished garment workers and they needed their three sons to go out and start earning money as early as they were able. Benny, the youngest, left school at fourteen to work as a 'printer's devil', running errands for a pair of newspaper compositors who worked shifts in and around Fleet Street.

On some evenings and at weekends he was additionally called upon to help Alf, who by then made his living from a steam press situated in the corner of a bedroom occupied by Benny's two brothers, Isaac and Cyril, until they both married and left home within a month of each other.

In his old age, Benny reminisced romantically about the East End. 'Everyone knew everyone,' he claimed. 'There was a great community spirit.' But, warmly recalled though it was, this 'community spirit' did not stop him from moving south of the River Thames, along with other family members and friends, just after he was demobilised from the army at the end of the Second World War, having married his childhood sweetheart.

Bertha Yanovsky's early years were spent in Chicksand Street across Brick Lane from Hanbury Street, where Benny Pomeranski grew up (and where, in 1888, the body of a victim of the most infamous of serial murderers, 'Jack the Ripper', was found in the backyard of one of the houses).

Bertha's mother and father were quieter and 'more respectable' than Benny's loud and fractious parents. Once Bertha and Benny were married, it was with her family's help that Benny, a quick learner, began to make a decent living. Bertha's father was in the 'rag trade', buying and selling cloth to tailors, and was able to introduce his new son-in-law to one or two useful and enterprising individuals.

Once he was in his stride, it wasn't long before Benny Pomeranski was himself at the heart of a very different bunch of enterprising individuals, one or two of whom had been his schoolmates and, like him, had migrated across the river. By this time, Benny had virtually discarded the people he'd met through his father-in-law – as he had in effect his two brothers, who had both become religious and, unlike Benny and his South London associates, lived in North London where they regularly attended synagogue. And when death rudely claimed, at the age of sixty, the elder, Isaac – who, on rare family get-togethers, had never missed the opportunity to express his disapproval of Benny's way of living – the 'low-life, Sabbath-breaking' youngest Pomeranski brother took no part in the arrangements for his funeral and didn't even attend it. Partly on account of his remorse at this, Benny later made sure that his other brother, Cyril, was given a lavish send-off when he died, not long afterwards.

Almost all of the 'Astorians', as Benny's new Brixton-based crowd were known, traded in 'swag' – mostly, though not exclusively, cheap and shiny commodities sold from shops, stalls or barrows within a mile radius of Atlantic Road and Electric Avenue, off the main Brixton Road. And, to Benny's elder brother Isaac's often-expressed contempt, not only did they bear a collective sobriquet, derived from the Astoria cinema at the Brixton end of Stockwell Road, but each of the gang also had his own personal moniker. This applied only to the males. Any females in the Astorian ambit were regarded, whether or not by marriage, as attachments, not members.

The Astoria cinema itself was an imposing yet enchanting domed building with an exotic Italianate interior featuring glittering artificial stars in an artificial sky – and a café, which became the meeting place of Benny Pomeranski and friends.

And, decades later, on that wintry November morning when Benny the Fixer was buried, among those paying their respects at the cemetery, long years after they had swaggered along London highways from Bethnal Green to Brixton, were group members Maxie the *Ganoff*, Fancy Goods Harry, Ralph Landau and Spanish Joe. Beyond the inner circle of Astorians, also in attendance were music trader Harvey Constant and tailor Henry Kenton – fellow shopkeepers in the arcade where Benny had owned a successful clothing business. Notable absentees included Sam the Stick, Joey the Boxer and Little Jack, two of whom had predeceased Benny in particularly dramatic fashion, while the third had simply taken himself off the Astorian playing field.

In those early Brixton days, Benny was the prime mover among the Astorians – indeed, the founder – but, while hardly a keeper of regular hours, he greatly valued his domestic life, too. And, as their income grew, he and Bertha (who accumulated quite a valuable collection of porcelain) greatly enjoyed bringing material comforts and possessions into their home. Initially, this comprised two floors of a three-storey Victorian terraced house. Eventually, when Benny acquired the freehold after their upstairs neighbour died, it was all three.

In the Pomeranski household, from their only child Simon's birth in 1946, Bertha strove to ensure that her son would get an education that would enable him to transcend his parents' way of life. While Benny supported her in this, he lacked Bertha's urgency over the matter. It never troubled him that he himself had left school at such a young age. He had always taken pleasure in 'making my own decisions, fending for myself'. In the East End Pomeranski milieu, the prospect, even the mere idea, of studying at a university or college was more than remote, and the young Benjamin Pomeranski was always happy to discover things for himself and pursue what he considered to be his best interests, so long as no obvious harm was done.

Both during and after his schooldays, Benny regularly borrowed novels from his local library and would read them at home in contented solitude. And, though poor, his parents proudly kept, in what they called their 'best', or sometimes just 'front', room, a pair of polished and well-stocked wooden bookshelves. The books on the shelves were, admittedly, dominated by religious and liturgical publications – central to which was a much-thumbed *Siddur* (prayer book), originally compiled by Reverend S. Singer for the 'Jewish Association for the Diffusion of Knowledge' – but Hetty Pomeranski would see to it that there was always at least one romance for her to read.

An early hero of Benny's was the American writer Jack London, two of whose books, *The Call of the Wild* and *White Fang*, Benny read more than once when he was sixteen. And, later, within the parameters of Benny's unconventional, not to say roguish, adult existence, he was satisfied with the knowledge that, even in his immediate South London locality, there was plenty of access to books, music and a variety of the kinds of cultural and leisure pursuits that interested him.

His young son, Simon, who was comfortably rather than determinedly at the top of his class in school, did not share his mother's soaring vision for his future. In his own dreams, Simon Pomeranski could think of few prospects more alluring than going into what became the family business – Pomeranski Gowns, a dress shop in Brixton market, situated in a former bakery that Benny had rented and developed.

Whenever Bertha or Benny took him to the shop, Simon was spellbound. He was dazzled by the whole circus of transaction: the sight, the smell and the *swish* of women buying, rejecting, or simply caressing the blouses, skirts and dresses; the different colours and textures of the clothes; and his father's quick-fire, irreverent interplay with customers, friends and the suppliers' representatives – the 'reps'. One of the latter, known as Spanish Joe, became a good friend of Benny's. The two men enjoyed a close but unlikely rapport, given the centrality to Benny's existence of his heterosexuality, and Spanish Joe's homosexuality to his.

Joe's real name was Joseph Pelovsky and he wasn't at all Spanish; all four of his grandparents came from Russia. He was given that appellation after the seven-year-old Simon Pomeranski, presumably wondering at the rep's dusky complexion and possibly his sibilant, high-pitched pronunciation of Yiddish (or maybe because Simon himself had recently been given a picture book about *The Pirates of the Spanish Main*), loudly asked Bertha, to much laughter from those present, 'Mummy, is that man Spanish?'

The Pomeranskis were popular and enjoyed genuine companionship with their neighbouring shopkeepers in Excelsior Arcade, the cavernous emporium between Electric Avenue and Coldharbour Lane where Pomeranski Gowns was situated on a central avenue.

Benny and Bertha were also at ease with the loud-voiced, muscular men from the manufacturers, who brought dresses, coats, skirts and slacks to the storage area behind the shop, carrying them over their shoulders in well-covered bundles that looked as though they contained human corpses.

Like most of their Brixton peers, the Pomeranskis paid close attention to their appearance. Benny wore good-quality suits, made by Henry Kenton, proprietor of Kenton Tailors, a couple of avenues away from Pomeranski Gowns within Excelsior Arcade, while Bertha exploited her connections with several clothing suppliers to keep up with women's fashion. She also went every week to Helena (Bertha never discovered her surname), an Austrian-Jewish refugee hairdresser with a salon close to the Astoria cinema, who always greeted Bertha with the same heavily accented phrase: 'Ah, here they are! Those lustrous locks, black as a raven's feathers!'

Benny, whose own abundant hair was of a similar shade, kept it oiled and orderly by going once a fortnight to a Greek barber shop a little further up Stockwell Road from Helena's. He also maintained a neat, thin black moustache. And on most working days he wore a white shirt and colourful silk tie.

Pomeranski Gowns was rarely quiet. Two, three or more of Benny's friends and associates could frequently be found in the generous 'private' rear area, irrespective of the number of customers at the front of the shop checking the garments hung in neat rows or laid out in open drawers. These friends and others included men who were funny, such as Spanish Joe, and others who were somewhat intimidating, like Benny's boyhood companion Samuel Golub – 'Sam the Stick' – whose nominal trade was ironmongery. They would hang around conspiratorially, making use of the chairs and table situated well behind the counter, drinking coffee, smoking cigars or American cigarettes and exchanging insults and wisecracks in English and Yiddish:

'Do me a favour, Spanish, you old *faygeleh*, stop being such a *schvunz*.'

'The man's a *schlemiel*, a *potz*.'

'I stick a knife in, you'll deflate, you fat *khazer*.'

'He should have a *groys gesheft* – a large business – and whatever people ask for, he shouldn't have, and what he does have, *nisht hobn* – it shouldn't be asked for!'

One memorably flamboyant character, who dropped in on the odd occasion for a sit-down and a cup of tea with a dash of whisky, was the self-styled Ras Prince Monolulu, an elderly horse-racing tipster who wandered the avenues of Excelsior Arcade – among many other paths, as he had done for years – loudly and repeatedly crying: 'I gotta horse!' This was in defiance of laws that marginalised gamblers and bookmakers before betting shops were made legal in the early 1960s.

Monolulu chided and ridiculed punters for betting on favourites and claimed to know the true form of lower-ranked horses – 'special outsiders' – who could and would beat the on-course bookies' favourites in big races. He sold his 'informed' predictions to customers for them to place a bet wherever they were able.

The first time he came into Pomeranski Gowns, he said: 'It is Saturday – the Sabbath – and there are more Jews here than there are in the synagogue this morning.'

'Here,' Benny responded, 'we have the not-so-bad Jews, and there, in the synagogue, they have the not-so-good Jews.'

The 'Ras Prince' claimed that he was a Black Jew with a Jewish wife somewhere in Africa. And he entertained Bertha and Benny, and whoever happened to be in the shop at the time, with such lively, sing-song assertions as 'the white man can have only one wife but the black man can have a hundred and run away'. Or 'only the white man can swim the Channel 'cos it's too cold for the black man.'

His inspiration, he said, was 'King Edward' (he meant Shakespeare's King Richard the Third) for the cry: 'A horse. A horse. My kingdom for a horse!'

Another occasional visitor to Pomeranski Gowns was Harvey Constant, the young proprietor of Excelsior Records, who in the 1960s specialised in new West Indian music. He was an improbably cultured product of a public-school education, despite his father being a racketeer and dubious club-owner.

Among others who gathered in the large carpeted area at the rear of Pomeranski Gowns, next to the revamped pair of cupboards that served as a changing room for customers, were dancers, singers and comedians, ventriloquists, conjurors and acrobats from the nearby Empress variety theatre.

An imperious late-Victorian building, the Empress was in many ways a symbol of Astorian life – a palace of make-believe, flamboyance, daring and *swank*. It was South London's major home of music hall and its stage was trodden by legions of performers from all parts of the country, as well as occasional star turns from America. It was where the First World War 'forces' sweetheart' Gertie Gitana gave her final stage performance in 1950. Benny went to the Empress as often as he could and befriended many performers, most of them from nearer the bottom than the top of the bill, and virtually all of them living in Brixton, at least temporarily.

One day, 'Spanish' Joe Pelovsky – who had quickly become Benny's favourite rep, 'because,' Benny explained to Bertha, 'he is witty and much cleverer than most of the other *schlemiels*' – came excitedly into Benny the Macher's dress shop and put down his briefcase (he needed both hands free to express what he wanted to say). 'Last night, at the Empress,' enthused Spanish Joe, 'I heard the most wonderful musician, a *schwarzer* yank trumpeter called Clifford Brown.'

'You were there?' Benny interrupted. 'So was I. Wasn't it just terrific? Little Jack, of all people,' he said, referring to a notorious local villain and exuberant businessman, 'told me about this trumpet genius. It turned out to be the biggest favour he's ever done for me. And all these years I never knew the Empress did jazz.'

'And I never knew you liked jazz.'

'What are you talking about? I love jazz.'

'Well, I never,' Joe said. 'So you also were lucky enough to listen to the brilliant sounds coming from that feller's trumpet. My God!' And the two men spent several minutes in joint praise of Clifford Brown before widening the subject into a catalogue of their shared musical tastes, a template for many future conversations.

It was on that hallowed square of carpet at the back of Pomeranski Gowns that 'Spanish' first met 'Pansy Potter' – the most unkind of the Astorian sobriquets and one that Benny frowned on – real name, Ralph Landau, who at that time was performing at the Empress his extraordinary act combining the violin, sword-swallowing and fire-eating with comedy and conjuring.

Sometimes, when an Empress show was closing and the performers moving on, or on somebody's birthday, Benny, or more rarely Bertha, would serve them and other guests cheap sherry, advocaat or cherry brandy in the rear area of the shop. Benny bought the booze at a hefty discount from the off-licence four doors away in Excelsior Arcade and he would pour it into tiny crystal glasses that had once belonged to his mother, Hetty.

Whenever the young Simon Pomeranski, between the ages of about nine and twelve, witnessed this ritual and breathed in the aromatic mixture of cigar smoke, alcohol and the scented aura of the Empress chorus girls, he was mesmerised.

Four

During those flashback days preceding his father's death, one memory that Simon Pomeranski had no need to excavate from the recesses of his mind, so vivid did it remain, was of the time, the only time, that Benny took Simon with him to watch an evening of professional boxing. This was in 1953 at Shoreditch Town Hall. It was an overwhelming, magical experience for a seven-year-old, the only child in a car with four adults.

The overriding reason for going that night was to see Harry Gilbert, a young Brixton-based Jewish lightweight fighter – who knew and was known by the Pomeranski family – in only his third professional contest after a successful career as an amateur.

Boxing was Benny's sport, insofar as he had one. Although he sometimes went to watch horse racing or greyhounds ('the dogs') or, much less often, football, it was only 'ringside' (a favourite word of his) where he felt truly comfortable. Even then, it wasn't primarily the sport that attracted him. He went for the atmosphere. He always knew people sitting around him – loud men with flashy suits and ornate ties, clipped moustaches, flushed faces dabbed with Eau de Cologne, and an ample repertoire of wisecracks and gestures of derision – and he felt at home among them.

The hum of laughter-punctuated chatter, the smell of cologne, sweat and embrocation, the cigarette smoke, the echoing public-address system, the roaring and stamping, all combined with the cushioned thumps of the licensed violence in the ring to produce a kind of euphoria. And the night that Benny took Simon with him turned out to be a thrilling occasion that nobody present would ever forget – all on account of Harry Gilbert's fight.

In the car, Sam the Stick sat in front next to Benny, who was driving. Simon was in the back with Joseph Campbell – Joey the Boxer – and his girlfriend, Sandra, a willowy blonde dancer. Simon was intoxicated by Sandra's perfume, and indeed her mere presence.

Joseph – Kid Joey – was a fighter of far greater experience and status than Harry Gilbert. He was also of a heavier weight category, veering between middleweight and light-heavyweight, and at that time was a contender for the British and European middleweight titles.

At seventeen, Joey had worked for 'Little Jack' Lewis in the latter's furniture store in Acre Lane, round the corner from the town hall in Brixton. But after a few months of Joey lifting, shifting and helping to deliver tables, chairs, beds and wardrobes, Little Jack, a keen boxing fan, moved him into a vacant flat above the shop and paid for him to be looked after by a professional boxing trainer.

The child of a West Indian father and an Irish mother, 'Joey the Boxer' was a inch or so under six feet tall, compact and powerfully built; a neat dresser in pale blue or grey suits with a plain red or blue tie. He had a broad nose with high, wide cheekbones and tight, curly and shimmering dark hair that, to the young boy Simon, always looked slightly wet.

On the journey that night from Brixton to Shoreditch, Benny hardly seemed aware of being at the wheel and kept up a garrulous torrent of conversation, turning his head to the left and squeezing Sam's knee or, to emphasise a point or break into laughter, throwing glances over his shoulder to the others in the back seat.

On arrival, Benny, Sam and Joey shook hands with scores of others. Following behind the adults, Simon had his hair ruffled by fingers that were fat and wore rings, or were slim, with painted nails, and all kinds of others in-between. Everybody seemed to want to welcome 'Benny's boy'. To Simon, it felt like a ceremonial induction. By the time he took his seat, his cheeks were smudged with lipstick and his eyes watered from cigar smoke.

Even more of a fuss was made of Joey. Old, bald, fat men hugged him to their sides. One even kissed him. Younger fellows slapped his back. Somebody from the press took a photograph of him with Sandra, who turned on an instant smile for the camera showing her shining red lips and pure white teeth to great advantage.

There was one moment of frisson, however, when, as the three men, the woman and the boy turned into the aisle in which their seats were located, a voice from behind them, that of 'Little Jack' Lewis, called out: 'Well, well, well, the one-and-only Joey C, on the *outside* of the ring.' And, as Benny and the others turned to face him, his greeting inevitably carried a sinister undertone: 'Hello Sam... Benny... And Benny's boy, eh? And who's this?'

'I'm with Joey,' Sandra replied.

'You need to watch him,' Jack told her, pointing to Joey and not entirely joking.

'Sandra, this is Jack Lewis,' Joey responded. 'He got me started in boxing.'

'And don't you forget it,' said Jack. 'I heard you had to leave your flat, Joey. Playing around with the landlord's wife, was it? I'll tell you where you might find a new place to live, right near the Excelsior arcade. Somerleyton Road. I found myself driving the Bentley down Somerleyton the other day and a load of kids, and some of their mums and dads, all came out to take a butcher's at my motor. S'pose they'd never seen anything like it. And, I swear to God, every one of them was a *schwarzer*. Not a single whitey in sight. You'd be in your element. Take my advice – like you always used to – get along to Somerleyton Road. They'd welcome a local champion like you with open arms down there. Enjoy the boxing, people. I hope Harry's on form. I've got quite a bit of *gelt* on him to win.'

And then he was gone, 'Little Jack' Lewis, who wasn't so little but was so-called because he had a six-foot-two, sixteen-stone cousin, also called Jack Lewis, in Ilford on the Essex side of London. The physically bigger Ilford Jack Lewis, had been put on probation just after the war, following a disturbance in a Mayfair night club. But the comparison, and certainly the nickname, was misleading. For it was the smaller Jack Lewis – furniture salesman, whisky connoisseur and jazz club owner – who was the more frightening. Much more frightening.

A few years older than Benny or Sam, Little Jack, whom Benny had got to know in the army during the war, had maintained a firm grip on most of the activities of South London's more felonious residents and miscreants for some time, and had made sure that any 'incomers' – including the Fixer, the Stick, and their associates – were on his radar. And attending boxing tournaments was one of his favourite ways of parading his bloated self-importance.

Harry Gilbert, who trained in the same boxing stable as Joey, based in a gymnasium on the high road between Brixton and Kennington, was a solid, thick-set fighter of about twenty. His dark hair was cropped close to his skull, giving him a suitably menacing appearance. He wore long black shorts with the Star of David embossed on them in white. Benny and the others were close enough to the ring for Harry to acknowledge their presence with a wink and a wave.

His opponent was a Scotsman with feathery red hair sticking up above a bumpy scarred face. In contrast to Harry, the Scot was tall and bony, with skin so white it looked painted.

The fight was an epic encounter, with each man fired by the other's aggression. From the first bell that sent them out of their corners like sprinters from starting blocks, they hurled themselves at each other. There was no pretence of skill, no 'science'. These were two fighting cocks. The noise was constant and tumultuous, a primitive force of nature into which loud, partisan support for either the canny, experienced Scot or the eager, youthful Jew was totally subsumed.

The spectators were caught up in an irresistible tide of feeling as one man's head jarred and sprang back from the shudder of a gloved fist while the other man swung wildly in pursuit. Raw red bruises appeared and spread darkly and alarmingly. The whole audience was on its feet. Joey and Sam were roaring their appreciation and encouragement. Even Sandra was involved, alternately covering her eyes with her hands or cheering and throwing her arms into the pitch-black smoke-filled air.

As for Benny, when the fight reached its astonishing climax, he was standing, roaring, his eyes alight and his mind oblivious to everything other than the battle with which he, too, was now joined. Simon, never having seen Benny in such a passionate state, was gazing open-mouthed at his father as much as he was watching what was going on in the ring.

By the seventh round, exhausted but still wriggling like a pair of goldfish, Harry Gilbert and the Scotsman were leaning on each other, their heads buried within the twisted ball that their two bodies had become. At this point, they looked more like wrestlers than boxers. Suddenly, however, they jerked apart. Harry, one swollen eye sealed up, came out of the clinch with an uppercut that met his opponent's chin. At the same precise moment that opponent's right hand completed a circling motion with a thud to the side of young Harry's head.

Both men dropped to the canvas. The referee crouched over them, looking anxiously out through the ropes. Lit up against the blackness by a beam of blinding light, he began counting. And counting. And counting. Neither man managed to get up in time. That was it – a double knockout. A 'one-in-a-million chance', as Benny put it. And when, shortly afterwards with the assistance of their trainers, the two fighters rose to their feet, they again fell into each other's arms, this time with a display of affection that almost matched their earlier hostility.

Benny was hoarse. Tears emerged in the corners of his eyes. He turned to Simon and said, 'Hello, son,' as if surprised to see him there. He stroked the side of his son's head and then, as the next two boxers, along with their 'seconds', took up their respective corner positions, Benny reverted to his normal level of enjoyment, not looking much at what was happening in the ring but revelling in the noise and the lights, the hugging and face-patting greetings and, at last, the slow, sauntering exit into the night with Sam, Joey and Sandra. Simon followed a little behind them, floating on an invisible cloud.

Five

Dorothy Estelle Green was born in 1924 in a small terraced house in Fashion Street in the East End of London, where, throughout her childhood, she came to the view that married life was one long fight. This was a view that hardened in adult life. For not only did her parents' marriage bear the trappings of a continuous battle, fairly quickly her own would, too.

As a young girl and an only child, Estelle, as she came to be known, grew profoundly distressed by the constant combat between her mother and father, to the extent that she would try to avoid being with them both at the same time. The only good times were when she was able to speak to them individually. Fortunately for her, it was comparatively easy to see either one of them alone as they clearly did not enjoy each other's company.

By the time she was ten years old, Estelle had become a kind of referee. In their separate conversations with their daughter, Edith and Alfred Green both tried to paint themselves as the more understanding parent, and indeed spouse, the one who was trying to hold the family together, while subtly implying that the other was the one causing problems.

'You mustn't get too angry with your father,' Edith told Estelle. 'Or be too upset when he behaves like a bit of a loudmouth. We both want what's best for you. We just have different ideas of what that is, that's all. He can't help shouting sometimes, your dad. Deep down, he realises that, because he's a man, he can't know what it's like being a woman – or a girl – and can't have a proper talk with you, like I can. About all sorts of things,' she added, wrinkling her nose and dropping her voice into a conspiratorial whisper. 'So, because he can't talk about things properly, in a girly or womanly way, he feels he has to shout. He can't help it. He's frustrated.'

'What does "frustrated" mean?' asked Estelle.

From the opposite parental standpoint, Alfred explained to his daughter, in his most reasonable tone, that, 'every now and again, your mum finds things too hard, so you need to help her. You know, with washing-up and all that. She's very... *delicate*... not strong, and sometimes cries. So that's when you have to help her the most. Don't tell her I told you. It'll be our little secret.'

Alfred Green had served in the East Surrey Regiment in the Great War and saw action in Belgium. He liked to crow about his exploits and, while the regulars at the Alma Pub in nearby Spelman Street were sceptical of some of his claims, at home his daughter was a captive listener. She believed everything he said about the war, and his part in it. She believed, too, that there were even more exciting stories to come.

'There are things I can't tell you until you are much older, my little girlie,' Alfred said, after describing, with an array of hand gestures, how he overcame a 'nasty German bully' in hand-to-hand combat.

'*Oh*, why not, Dad?' was little Estelle's response. 'I'm a big girl.'

'Of course you're a big girl, my darling, but I can't tell you everything yet. When you're even bigger, you'll have more room in your brain to take in the stuff that your little girlie head doesn't have room for now. I've seen things that would make you have bad dreams and we don't want that, do we?'

Alfred claimed to have personally killed more than twenty enemy soldiers in one day over a period of a few hours, and seen a far, far greater number of his comrades slaughtered by rifle or machine-gun fire. The latter was certainly true. What was also true was that he still possessed a gun – a pistol – years after the war had ended. He kept it locked away in a drawer underneath the bed he shared with Estelle's mother Edith in their Fashion Street home.

Estelle loved all of Alfred's gun talk and was agog with excitement when, very early one morning, she saw her father shoot a rat in the yard at the back of the house.

It was soon after dawn and Estelle was awoken by a clatter of what sounded like pots and pans outside the window of the room where she slept. She got out of bed and gently opened the curtain a few inches. She heard her father talking – apparently to himself – before she saw him. 'Damn you, you little bugger,' he said loudly. And then, there he was, standing in the yard, wearing his army greatcoat and slippers and straining his eyes to look for whatever 'little bugger' it was that had fled so noisily from behind the dustbin. And, in Alfred's left hand, was… a gun.

He tiptoed away from the house and, all at once, Estelle saw a long-tailed creature scurry across the yard, heard her father cry out again – 'ah, there you are, you little bugger' – and saw and heard him fire the pistol. The furry, whiskery creature skidded to a halt and rolled on to its side as Alfred went and stood over it before firing another shot to complete the execution.

Later that day, Edith slapped her daughter's face, having caught her clambering under her parents' bed trying to open the drawer into which Estelle had seen her father lock away his pistol once he had disposed of the slaughtered rodent. Edith screamed: 'You must never touch that!' – and was immediately contrite for having hurt her daughter. She desperately hugged Estelle to her, intoning, over and over again: 'What are we going to do, you and I, what are we going to do, my love?'

After that, Estelle confined her fascination with guns to the school playground, emulating her father's boastfulness in telling the boys, in particular, that she'd seen her dad kill a rat with a gun in their 'garden'. At home, she kept her preoccupation to herself and never again tried to get at the pistol in the drawer, though she almost hoped that some big, bad robber would one day try to break into their home so that her father – or, in a more extreme fantasy, she herself – could shoot him. And when, in the mid-1930s, Alfred Green deserted the family, taking his gun with him, Estelle mourned the loss of the weapon almost as much as she missed her father.

She entered her teens clever, pretty, with curly blonde hair, and a favourite of her teachers and classmates alike. At the end of the last spring term, Edith came to see Estelle's class teacher, Mrs Ainsworth, who was pleased to tell Edith that not only had her daughter developed into a skilful singer and dancer, but also that she had been chosen for the starring role in the show at the end of that school year.

Furthermore, Mrs Ainsworth revealed that she would arrange – with Edith's permission – for Estelle to have singing lessons in the holidays with the 'renowned' Miss Marigold Bartholomew.

Miss Bartholomew's solid Victorian house, which smelled of beeswax and furniture polish, was just over a mile from Edith and Estelle's home. Edith walked there with her daughter for the first two lessons. After that, Estelle asked her mother not to come any more as Edith was embarrassing her by weeping and sniffing and having to wipe her eyes, overcome with emotion at the sight and sound of her only child singing under the tutelage of a professional music teacher.

By the end of the Second World War, Estelle was picking up paid singing jobs here and there and, when she married Robert Davis, the son of a neighbour in Fashion Street, she entered a period of post-war happiness. She told people that part of her bridegroom's attraction was that he had served as a rifleman, something that Robert himself wished to forget in the war's aftermath but she wouldn't let him.

They managed to rent a small flat in Bermondsey near Tower Bridge – the landlord favoured ex-servicemen – and, within a year, had a daughter, Gloria. As the little girl grew, her parents often clashed over Estelle's habit of buying 'boys' toys', including guns, for little Gloria and, in order to do so, taking money from the small amount of cash she earned from singing with local dance bands.

A frequent, increasingly drink-fuelled refrain that echoed through the Bermondsey flat was: 'What is the matter with you? Why do you keep getting cowboy guns and things? And toy soldiers! You want your daughter to be a lezzie?' And the answer would be along the lines of: 'Leave me alone. I buy her the things she asks for. She deserves the odd treat. I am not forcing anything on her.'

Sometimes, by contrast, when Estelle was home on a summer's Friday evening, she and Robert would go to the Angel pub, on Bermondsey Wall, taking Gloria with them so that she could play with other local children outside in the pub courtyard, at the edge of which was a stall where a white-coated seafood vendor would periodically call out, to pub customers and passers-by alike, 'Whelks and winkles *for yer*!'

In those days, Estelle could sit nursing a port and lemon for hours. Robert, however, would drink two pints of beer in fairly quick succession before yelling at his daughter to stay near the door where he could see her or, on one drunken occasion, in a voice loud enough to compete with the whelks-and-winkles man, urging his wife to join in, with him, a sing-song issuing from the far side of the public bar, which she was very reluctant to do.

'Come on Estie. Wassamadder, lost your voice? I thought you're s'posed to be a singer,' he slurred. 'Too common are we? Not good enough? 'Ave you forgotten I sang this song to you when we first met?' And, as he strolled with a kind of scornful defiance towards where a cluster of regulars were enthusiastically vocalising a part-sung, part-shouted version of the early-twentieth-century ballad 'Nellie Dean', Robert added, almost to himself, 'You didn't hold back then...'

> *And you pinned a rose of red*
> *On my coat of blue and said*
> *That a soldier boy you'd wed, Nellie Dean...*

Later, when Estelle cast her net wider in search of singing work, often taking Gloria with her – partly to help her ward off the constant propositioning she experienced in some of the more sleazy pubs and clubs – Robert Davis's drinking became more serious and he found it difficult to get himself up in the mornings, and sometimes afternoons, for his job working shifts at the Sarson's vinegar factory on Tower Bridge Road. Nevertheless, though the couple's divisions deepened, they continued to live under the same roof.

By the time she met Benny Pomeranski, however, in the summer of 1952, she and her husband had long been effectively leading separate lives. Much of the time, she was far away from home singing for her supper well into the night. She had an extended booking in a club in Richmond that lasted for just over two weeks, from which she rarely returned home before dawn.

Even so, she continued to see that her daughter got to school in the morning, except on occasions when she took Gloria with her to an out-of-London job. Even then, she insisted the girl sat for hours doing homework in a library or at a kitchen or 'dressing' table in what Estelle called her 'theatrical digs'. Robert, meanwhile, remained at the Bermondsey flat, though he did spend some time in Guy's Hospital with alcoholic poisoning.

When he was discharged, he immediately began drinking again and, if Gloria was at home on her own in the evenings, she hid in her room whenever he eventually came back to the house swearing drunkenly. And even after he had gone to bed and sunk into an alcohol-induced sleep, he would sometimes call out in the grip of a nightmare, waking and frightening his daughter.

Gloria implored Estelle to take her away from there. In turn, Estelle, having landed a job as a hostess at a Mayfair nightclub, begged her mother, Edith, who was living alone in a small flat in Willesden, to allow Gloria to come and stay with her.

'I needn't have begged,' Estelle would recall later to her workmate Ruth. 'My mum said, "Gloria? Come and live with me?" "Please, Mum," I said. "*Please!*" And then the cheeky expression on her face was like the sun slowly coming out. "Of course she can," she said, grinning. And so Gloria made Grandma's flat her base. They were like two friends, going shopping, watching TV together. Companions. Until I got that phone call from Gloria: "Mummy," she said, "I can't wake Grandma Edith."'

Six

Estelle Davis met Ruth Ellis in the early 1950s, by which time, having parted from Robert, she and Gloria had moved to Brixton. Estelle and Ruth both worked a couple of seasons at the Sly Fox club, in Mayfair, owned by the bumptious Monty Berman, a heavily built man who threw his weight around both figuratively and literally. He rarely spoke to others unless he wanted something from them and, if and when he was given it, usually wouldn't thank them. Monty employed Estelle and Ruth as hostesses. Ruth, although almost two years younger than Estelle, was the senior hostess – but then Monty heard Estelle sing.

Soon after they'd met, Estelle had told Ruth about her experiences 'doing a few performances at a jazz club in Richmond, owned by a sleazy gangster who was always trying to get me into his private office, where he also held meetings with his thuggish underlings – and also, apparently, acted as a kind of agony aunt, helping these dummies with their "problems". Believe me, Ruth, these were the type of people who *give* you problems.'

And she went on to talk about a job she'd had the previous year performing for the punters at a fancy, expensive restaurant in a smart street not five minutes from the Sly Fox. At which point, Ruth leaned forward and whispered to Estelle: 'Talking about sleazy club owners, look…' Monty had arrived, bang on cue.

'Ah, the blondes!' Monty, laughing, interrupted in his usual noisy, coarse fashion, putting an arm around Ruth. 'Opposites attract, eh Ruthie?'

'Actually, Monty, I'm only blonde from a bottle,' said Ruth. 'Underneath, I'm almost as dark as you are. Maybe that's just one of the reasons why I'm not attracted.'

'Very funny.' Monty smiled his Machiavellian smile and turned his attention to Estelle. 'I overheard what you were saying. So, you're a bit of a songstress? And for that poncey so-called chef round the corner. That crook from the East End with his made-up French moniker. His family came over from Russia! He was taught to cook by his mother, Tamara. His old man did odd jobs in Whitechapel. I bet he never told you any of all that, did he? His real name does sound a bit French. It's something like "Andry". But he's about as French as a Russian salad. *André Lafond*? Do me a favour.'

'*What?*' Estelle's eyebrows rose simultaneously with her mouth falling open. 'You're kidding me!'

'No I'm not, darling,' said Monty. 'I can remember his old man. Nice old geezer. Probably never heard of France, let alone lived there. But, listen, if you really can sing, there might be a few bob in it for you. I've been thinking of bringing in a bit of music at the Fox. Maybe two or three nights a week. Matter of fact, I was talking about it with my sister's husband, Davy, only last night. He just got laid off by the BBC. Fiddler, he was, in the BBC Opera Orchestra. Straight up. BBC Opera Orchestra. B.O.O. Boo! You don't believe me, do you? I can see by your face. Honestly. He's been on the radio *hundreds* of times. If you want to pop in Monday afternoon – it's your day off anyway, right? About four. We'll have a listen to you.'

The following Monday, another surprise – to be added to the revelation of restaurateur André's true identity – awaited Estelle in the utterly unexpected appearance and personality of Monty Berman's violin-playing brother-in-law.

Unlike the large and raucous Monty, Davy Greenhouse was slight, bespectacled and self-effacing. He spoke quietly, in a soft Mancunian accent, and avoided eye contact, even when he smiled. And, although he had brought along his violin to Estelle's impromptu audition, he was seated, ready to accompany her, at the Sly Fox's unused and hitherto hidden piano – which Monty had ordered to be dragged out, cleaned, repaired and tuned. Uncharacteristically, he didn't flinch or attempt to negotiate when the piano repairer reported, 'It'll be quite dear, Mr Berman. You need new strings for a start.' Monty even asked for the elderly instrument to be doubly polished 'until the surface looks like a mirror.'

Estelle decided to direct her performance at Davy. She stood at the back of the piano, facing him, mischievously projecting her lips as she sang:

> For nobody else gave me a thrill
> With all your faults, I love you still...

Davy barely looked up from the keyboard but maintained a shy smile as Estelle grew in confidence. Finally, as he drew his fingers along the keys in a closing flourish, he managed to look at her as she brought the performance to a conclusion – *It had to be you-hoo* – holding the note, her arms outstretched. Davy nodded his approval, to which Estelle responded with a slow, stagey wink.

'She's good,' Davy said gently, more to himself than to Monty. And, the following month, the Sly Fox club introduced 'Cabaret Time' three nights a week, built around Estelle Davis, directed by Davy Greenhouse with occasional support from one or more jobbing musicians.

Monty Berman invited as many of his friends and acquaintances he could think of to come along to the opening night. These included Benny and Bertha Pomeranski.

'Did you see that *shprauncy* invitation from Monty Berman?' Benny asked Bertha one Friday evening as she sat at the kitchen table peeling onions and putting them in a huge pot containing an array of vegetables around a chicken carcass. 'He's very excited about a new singer he's promoting, one of his own girls working at the club, right under his own nose.'

'Yes, I'll bet he's excited,' said Bertha, cutting off the top of a carrot. 'One of his girls? One of his tarts, more like. You think I want to spend an evening listening to such a creature whose voice probably sounds like she's swallowed a pack of razor blades? Do me a favour.'

'Monty's brother-in-law Davy says she's really good,' Benny pleaded. 'And he's a decent judge. A proper musician. A sensitive man, not a fat *shtarker* like Monty. Or a loud *yachna* like Monty's sister – Davy's wife,' Monty added in a disbelieving tone. 'I'll never understand how Davy Greenhouse came to marry Netta Berman.'

'Maybe for the same reason Monty married Hilda,' Bertha sniped, alluding to the birth of the Bermans' elder daughter Carol at an unfeasibly early point in their marriage.

'Of course it wasn't. It must've been at least a year – or more – before Davy and Netta's first kid was born. Come on, let's go and see this new singing sensation. Let your hair down for a change,' urged Benny, trying to raise his wife's spirits. 'You might enjoy it. Angela can look after Simon,' he suggested, referring to the seventeen-year-old girl next door who performed baby-sitting duties for pocket money.

'I don't think so.' Bertha was quietly emphatic. 'Why don't you go without me? I'm not so keen on that jazz music at the best of times.'

Benny, who was keen on 'jazz music' at the best and worst of times, found himself on Cabaret Time's opening night placed at a table in privileged proximity to the Sly Fox club's stage. He was seated next to his old friend Sam 'the Stick' Golub, whose eponymous walking staff was placed carefully along the floor by the side of his chair. On Benny's right-hand side sat the quietest Astorian, Max Baskin, known as Maxie the Ganoff. Facing them, on the other side of the table, were Estelle's friend and off-duty managing hostess Ruth Ellis and her current boyfriend David Blakely.

Also at the table was Netta Greenhouse, wife of Davy, Estelle's musical director and accompanist, alongside an empty seat to be occupied by her brother Monty in between his making announcements and checking that everything was going smoothly backstage. Like Bertha, Monty's wife Hilda stayed at home – in Hilda's case 'convalescing'. 'Seventeen operations, my missis has had,' Monty told anyone who'd listen. *'Seventeen!'*

Estelle had chosen a Rodgers and Hart song to open with, one that she always liked singing and which Davy also felt at ease with on the piano. Going straight into it before speaking to the audience, Estelle felt her nervousness evaporate. Her confidence had also been boosted by a visit to Ruth Ellis's hairdresser who, according to Ruth, 'specialises in blondes' and did indeed enhance Estelle's natural colouring – in contrast to Ruth's artificial shade.

Afterwards, to Bertha, Benny would play down the evening's impact on him, telling her how Sam fell asleep, Maxie told old jokes that he had heard a hundred times, Netta kept giggling and Ruth Ellis's boyfriend David Blakely 'went on and on about "motors" and loudly boasted about having a racing car of his own.' As for the singer, Estelle Davis: 'Yes, she was good. Nice voice. One or two wrong notes, but generally quite polished.'

By contrast, to his friend – jazz fan and fellow aficionado of the 'Great American Songbook', Spanish Joe – Benny offered a much more eager report. 'I couldn't believe we were sitting in that seedy old club,' he said. 'The atmosphere was special. Calm and warm, but also exciting. When the lights went out, the chatter stopped immediately and there were several seconds of silence before the show started.

'We were all sitting there wondering what the singer was going to be like. I asked Estelle Davis's friend, Ruth, the hostess at our table, if her friend Estelle was any good. "Oh yes," she said, "and I should know; I'm very musical. My dad used to play the cello." Judging by the amount of gin she was knocking back, I doubt if she could tell one note from another. I just smiled.

'Then out comes this female, Estelle. A real looker, believe me, with *the* sexiest mouth,' Benny told Spanish Joe. 'From the moment she walked up to the microphone and opened that sexy mouth and *breathed* rather than sang the first words, I could not take my eyes off her. It was "My Heart Stood Still". You must know it,' Benny said, and sang, quite tunefully, at which Spanish Joe – 'of course I know it' – joined in:

I took one look at you
That's all I meant to do…

'I felt she was singing to me personally and I bet every man in the room felt the same – even you might've done,' Benny added, and the two men laughed at such an unlikely prospect. 'But really, Joe, my tongue was hanging out. She had a way of singing that was so… *enticing*. I was *captivated*.' Benny always took delight in using words that stood out from the regular lingo of the Brixton crowd, especially when he was passionate about something – or somebody.

Seven

Little Jack Lewis beamed as, cigar in mouth, he approached the bandstand, to which the musicians had just returned after a tea break. He had his arm around his son Ronnie ('Aaron ben Yaakov') who had endured months of lessons – and now, the limelight – in order to put that smile upon his father's face.

The day before, Ronnie had been given pride of place in Brixton Synagogue, notwithstanding the thin, reedy voice in which he sang his thirteen-year-old way into Jewish 'manhood'. And now, this evening, in the ballroom of the Victory Rooms, Tottenham Court Road, in that same voice, he had just given a speech that his mother, Renée, had written for him.

Little Jack released his hold on Ronnie and stepped up on to the bandstand. He tapped the microphone to gain the attention of the two hundred or more guests, the more jaded of whom, at the end of an immoderately protracted six-course meal, were sipping tea and popping pastries into their mouths because they could think of nothing else to do. Others were drinking brandy or liqueurs with the bravado and relish of the only-on-special-occasions drinker.

'Ladies and gentleman, and especially our bar mitzvah boy, Ronnie,' Little Jack announced, having removed the cigar from his mouth. His chest swelled inside his expensive, silky dinner jacket. His straight black hair was smoothed down either side of a pencil-line parting. His moustache was neatly trimmed. His cheeks and forehead looked as though they had been waxed and polished. 'Let us welcome back our fabulous band,' he urged, replacing the cigar in his mouth in order to applaud feverishly.

The previous day, in the synagogue, Jack had made equally exaggerated gestures of welcome as guests and worshippers filed in from the Saturday-morning drone of traffic in Effra Road and Brixton Hill. As the synagogue had filled up, it seemed to shrink, while Little Jack at its centre, wrapped in a huge prayer shawl, appeared to swell. And, when his only son chanted a portion of the holy law, standing awkwardly on the podium – the *bimah* – Jack tightened his lips and dabbed at his eyes. Now, however, at this lavish dinner and ball to celebrate Ronnie's admission into the numbers of Jewish males able to pray together in public, Jack parted his lips and wore an expression of utter rapture.

The liveried master of ceremonies reclaimed the microphone from the host and, with practised emphasis, announced a surprise. The band and its leader, Mr Kenny Lee, were delighted, the MC told the assembled company, to welcome a guest vocalist to the stage. He then stretched out a scarlet-uniformed arm and, from the crowd, up stepped Estelle Davis. She briefly consulted Kenny Lee, who nodded and smiled and then struck up the seven-piece ensemble with a flick of his hands.

Estelle adopted a plaintive expression. She had done this before and looked completely in charge. She was wearing long satin gloves, which commanded attention as she waved her arms to represent the emotions of the song. She was treating her expectant audience to Gershwin, something special to present at – as embossed on the invitations – the 'Banquet and Ball to mark the occasion of the Bar mitzvah of Master Aaron Lewis'.

Throwing her gloved arms around without restraint, Estelle displayed an extravagance and artifice that was at odds with the pure, simple force of her voice.

Someday he'll come along, the man I love. The bandleader, Kenny Lee, hunched his shoulders, exhorting his players to greater effort.

And he'll be big and strong, the man I love. Estelle pointed theatrically at Ronnie, who obligingly flexed his biceps.

And when he comes my way – holding out both arms to Ronnie – *I'll do my best to make him stay.* The applause was thunderous.

A week before Little Jack's son's bar mitzvah, Estelle had sung the same song, without the flailing mannerisms, at Jack's Richmond riverside jazz club, Jax, accompanied by a pianist, percussionist, woodwind and double-bass.

Sitting at a table reserved for club staff was one of Little Jack's lieutenants, a brawny ex-sailor, speaking to 'Trixie Dawn', real name Shirley Dawson, a dyed-platinum-blonde hostess trying to be Marilyn Monroe. They were both smoking – and drinking, especially Shirley, who, seemingly oblivious to Estelle Davis's singing, every so often contrived to emit a high-pitched giggle, which she imagined was how Marilyn Monroe sounded.

As Estelle finished her song, the couple at the staff table were joined by Little Jack, who put his arm around the tipsy Trixie in much the same way as he would place it around his son's shoulders a week later. Except that, here in the club, he wasn't smiling. He led her away from the table, brushing aside her half-hearted apologies for 'making a noise' while Estelle was singing.

'I hear you like collecting money,' Jack whispered in Trixie Dawn's ear with snake-like intimacy. 'But you don't seem to understand why you got it, and who for. You don't know how to share it. And now,' he said, as he ushered her upstairs to his office, 'you're going to find it hard to count it.'

Although Little Jack was an emotional man, given to weeping in public, his business methods could be hard and calculating. And while the jazz club was a loss-making passion project, his furniture business in Brixton's Acre Lane – his 'legit *gesheft*' – was well-run and successful. And his illegitimate 'extra-curricular' interests (in which Trixie was among those who participated) brought handsome profits. But he hated to think that anyone might take advantage of him. And when he thought somebody needed to be taught a lesson, he used a hammer or, for more egregious offences, employed somebody to exact retribution with a razor, knife or gun.

Out front, on the Jax stage, Estelle had given way to a pair of additional instrumentalists to augment those who had accompanied her, and the building was shaking with a blast of full-blown jazz. The new configuration of heard-it-all-before musicians masked the screams, behind and above them, of a young, blonde, left-handed woman having the knuckles of her left index finger and the one next to it broken by a hammer-wielding man soon to stand tearfully alongside his son on the podium of a house of God.

Eight

Cabaret Night was probably the best idea Monty Berman ever had. After a mere two or three weeks, word got around that its addition of musical performance had lifted the seedy old Sly Fox out of the doldrums. Monty did his best to take the credit for this unlikely phenomenon but even a man of his blinkered self-importance could not ignore the effect of his brother-in-law Davy Greenhouse's musical knowhow and his lavish praise for Estelle Davis: 'There's cheering every time she takes her curtain bow.' Curiosity quickly spread about the Fox's 'little blonde songbird' with the vocal capacity to blow away anybody's cobwebs.

And, although Monty's first reaction to Estelle having had 'the temerity' to ask for an increase in her pay was to lecture her about the 'high financial cost' of running 'a top leisure and entertainment business in one of the smartest parts of London', he relented somewhat by offering to help get her fitted out with a couple of brand-new dresses that would see her through a season's singing.

The cost, he announced in a mock-formal, playfully pompous voice, would be fully paid by 'Montague Berman himself, owner of the exclusive Sly Fox establishment, Mayfair.' These 'posh garments' would be supplied by Pomeranski Gowns of Brixton – 'West End quality at South London prices'.

'It'll have to be Wednesday afternoon, after I've closed the shop,' Benny said when Monty phoned to reveal that he'd made this 'most generous gesture' to his Cabaret Night star.

'I can't do it during opening hours,' Benny explained. 'We're far too busy. But, for you, Monty, and your lovely lady soloist, I'll sort out something special. You don't want to palm her off with anything cheap. I certainly don't intend to. And I presume you're doing this instead of putting up the *farshtinkener* wages you pay her.'

'What are you talking about? You've got no idea what I pay her. Listen, by my life, it's not at all bad, especially when you consider I've also got to keep Davy happy – and the other musicians he books or brings along from time to time.'

'Yes, but Davy is certainly not charging you much, is he? He's family. *Mishpocha*. He's more or less retired and he loves what he does – accompanying a quality vocalist. And though I may not know what you pay Estelle Davis, I do know *you*, you old fox. But, look, I'm sure we can sort something out. Get her to give me a call early Wednesday afternoon to tell me she's on her way.'

'That's fine. But remember I can't afford any of your expensive fashion-model numbers.'

'Sure, sure. I'll sort out a few nice frocks for her to choose from. You know I give good value.'

Benny relayed the conversation to Bertha and asked her if she wanted to make the dress selection with Estelle. 'You know I can't,' she said, reminding him she was going to visit her sister in Waltham Abbey that Wednesday. 'I'm going to Louise's. She just came out of the hospital at the weekend. You think I should not see my sister, who is unwell, just to sell a couple of dresses to Monty's tarty warbler? You can do it. And be careful she doesn't get her claws into you.'

Benny forced out a laugh and protested that Bertha was being unfair. 'Remember, I've heard her sing a couple of times. She's very good and Monty's Cabaret Nights are packed. Thanks maybe to Davy Greenhouse, that 'tarty warbler' is building a reputation. She'll outgrow Monty Berman's foxhole. You should come and listen for yourself one time.'

'You know I don't like that kind of music. And, as for Wednesday, you're a big boy, I'm sure you'll manage.'

Bertha didn't come to the shop at all that Wednesday, not even in the morning. She was anxious to get to Waltham Abbey earlier than usual after she heard her sister sounding 'frail and sickly' on the telephone. Benny was also early, arriving at Pomeranski Gowns an hour before his normal time. Once he'd unlocked the door, he went straight to the back of the shop, opened the cupboard in which he kept drinks and glasses, and poured himself a whisky. He sipped from the glass and said, aloud, though nobody was around to listen: 'This is the earliest I've had a drink in the daytime since I left the army.' And, raising his glass to the wall: 'To the lovely Estelle Davis!'

He then spent a pleasurable hour holding up individual dresses in what he guessed would be Estelle's size, pausing at each one to envisage her wearing it. Eventually, having carefully laid half-a-dozen across the divan alongside the rear wall, he pulled up the shutters covering the display window and Pomeranski Gowns was open for business.

The morning passed relatively smoothly. He sold three colourful summer dresses in similar patterns, three blouses, two pairs of 'slacks' and, most satisfyingly, a profit-boosting bejewelled 'cocktail' dress. Later, as the vintage grandfather clock in the watchmaker's kiosk directly opposite Benny's shop chimed the half-hour past noon, without any customers around he decided to lock up early and read the copy of Graham Greene's novel *Brighton Rock* that he had started the night before in bed at home.

About an hour later, the telephone rang and, as Benny moved across the shop floor to pick up the receiver, he imagined he could see Estelle, standing in the black, tight-fitting dress he'd left at the bottom of the pile he intended to show her – and hear her voice, husky and melodious, singing to him. As he recited the shop's phone number and his name into the mouthpiece, he pulled open a drawer in the chest upon which the phone stood and took out a packet containing a pair of slinky black stockings.

And it was indeed Estelle on the other end of the line. 'Benny? I hope to be with you soon. I can't wait to see those dresses,' she said. 'I'm so excited. I feel like Peggy Lee.' And then: 'Is it all right to bring my daughter with me? She's off school today and not feeling too good. She'll be quiet. I'll bring a few things from home to keep her amused. Will that be okay?'

'Sure. Of course,' Benny said, trying hard not to convey his disappointment. 'I look forward to seeing you… both.'

'Thank you ever so much, Benny, see you soon.'

'Terrific! Most of the shops are closed but the Coldharbour Lane entrance to the arcade is open. Just walk straight through to our avenue. I'll unlock the shop door.'

After replacing the phone, Benny sighed, took the black stockings to the divan, laid them carefully on top of the black dress and, as if addressing the neatly assembled layers of silky and satin items, said to his absent, imminent guest, 'So now we have to keep your little girl amused. I was hoping *you* were going to keep *me* amused.'

In the event, Gloria, Estelle's daughter, was kept entertained by the fashion show that her mother's trying-on of nine or ten dresses turned into. The adults, too, created and enjoyed a kind of private charade, Benny as a flamboyant master of ceremonies,

Estelle striking a series of catwalk poses from pouting vamp to ice goddess.

The play-acting and humorous mood intensified. Pomeranski Gowns reverberated to their laughter. Towards the end of the afternoon, Gloria went to the toilet, while Estelle – at last wearing the black dress – stepped out of the changing cubicle complaining that the dress's zip was stuck. Benny leaned forward and unhooked and slightly pulled *down* the zip.

Estelle was still laughing at Benny's mock introduction of her as 'Jane Russell at last achieving her dream of displaying her talents in Brixton'. He put his arms around her waist from behind and lightly kissed her cheek. She turned to him and, the laugh becoming a smile, said, 'I've had so much fun, Benny. So has Gloria.' And, softly pressing her closed lips against his before hastily drawing back at the sound of Gloria flushing the toilet, she whispered, 'Imagine if it had been just the two of us.'

At their parting, Estelle told Gloria to thank 'Uncle Benny' for making them laugh, and, looking into Benny's face, said in a meaningful way, 'That's what really counts – making a woman laugh.'

'I'm glad you enjoyed yourselves,' Benny said, throwing a quick glance towards Gloria. And then, to Estelle: 'I'll get your choices over to Monty at the club on Friday. But take these now,' he added, handing her the stockings.

As she thanked him, her eyes blazed into his.

Nine

Whitechapel-born Samuel Golub was a disobedient, assertive child, possibly in reaction to constantly being laughed at and pushed around by his three elder brothers. His father was a tailor, religiously observant but with a penchant for gambling; his mother worked in a cigar factory.

The pattern of Samuel's life was established on a sunny autumn afternoon in the East End of London in 1932, when he was twelve years old. He and his friend Benjamin Pomeranski were wandering along Commercial Road, 'seeking adventure' as Benjamin's mother Hetty fancifully put it.

As they were passing an open-air greengrocer's stall with its wares on plentiful display, Benjamin mischievously brushed his fingers along a line of apples neatly arranged on a tray. Samuel laughed and went one better, snatching an apple. Challenged, Benjamin took up a shiny example of a Cox's Orange Pippin and held it to his mouth. Both boys then took a bite from their apples and ran away across the road.

'Hey, you!' The stallholder stopped serving a customer and shouted after the two boys. 'Come back, you lousy little thieves.' Brandishing his fist, he strode to the kerb as if to pursue the light-fingered youths but he was conscious of a customer waiting by the stall, a fashionably dressed woman who had filled a stiff paper carrier bag with potatoes, onions and other vegetables. 'I'm very sorry, madam,' he said with a quick bow of his head. 'Perishin' kids. They deserve a wallopin'.'

'I wonder if their parents know what they're getting up to,' the customer remarked. Three other women waiting to be served hummed and tutted sympathetically. 'My best Cox's they are,' the greengrocer grumbled, nodding his head at the purloined apple tray, in the hope that the customers waiting to pay would be moved to add a couple of apples to their shopping baskets and bags.

Meanwhile, having crossed the road, Samuel and Benjamin, believing they were being chased by the irate stallholder and probably other civic-minded and quite possibly burly adults, continued running along Commercial Road. Benny was ahead, propelled by his fear of being caught, which appeared to be completely lacking in Sam, who, exhilarated, was laughing as he weaved semicircles across the wide street, the threat of motor traffic as much of a dangerous thrill as the chase itself.

Benny was heading for the relative safety of Cavell Street and, after a couple of minutes, ran back across the main road towards it. The road was clear and quiet but behind him, suddenly and alarmingly, he heard a scream. He felt both the bloody taste of terror and a flush of recognition rise to his throat and face. Turning, he saw a crowd gathering around a twelve-year-old boy, a half-eaten apple next to him in the road. The boy had been a little too careless and caught his foot in the open tram-line, twisting it round grotesquely as he fell at the approach of a braking tram.

Samuel Golub would spend months in hospital, where his pious father sat with him most days taking over his Hebrew schoolteacher's role and, towards the end, preparing him for his bar mitzvah, when the little ruffian would, at thirteen, implausibly 'become a man'. It was feared that the leg would be amputated below the knee but that at least was avoided, although young

Samuel found it severely painful to walk for a few weeks. He would eventually leave school at fifteen and, after helping his father in his tailoring shop for a short period, become more withdrawn from those near to him and increasingly reckless in his behaviour.

He went from job to job, not all of them legal. Gradually, he built up an acceptable living from selling household items such as buckets, mops, matches, firelighters, washing lines, clothes pegs, kettles, plates and 'steel wool', first from a stall, then a shop, then another.

Sam and Benny kept in touch during the Second World War, even though Sam was deemed unfit to serve. He was disappointed by this, very much wanting to fight. He tried to demonstrate to a gruff and dismissive recruiting officer how quick and nimble he was and that his lameness would not hold him back on the battlefield, but was unable to convince the man, whose patience very quickly expired.

Instead, Sam developed a very individual style of dancing, which he put into practice when Benny was on leave from his war service and the two of them went out together with, or in search of, female company. And should anybody laugh at Sam's dance-floor cavortings, as happened on two or three occasions, Benny had to hold his friend back from delivering a beating, which usually produced an apology from Sam's taunters.

Just once, when Benny wasn't around, Sam grabbed a tall, pale sailor by the tie and bloodied the shocked man's nose with a hard, deliberate aim of his forehead. Sam was given vocal support by his dancing partner and childhood friend Joyce Ruben who reinforced the irony of the situation by telling Sam's adversary to 'leave him alone, you big bully'.

A year after the end of the war, that same Joyce Ruben would become Sam Golub's bride, two years almost to the day after her best friend Bertha Yanovsky married Benny Pomeranski. By then, Sam had begun to establish a new pots-and-pans business across the river in Brixton's Excelsior Arcade, where Benny, too, was looking to exploit one of the many opportunities that seemed to be emerging.

Sam Golub didn't need to steal things, which is what he also did. But he did appear to need the excitement that breaking the law gave him. And, by now, he also needed a walking stick permanently in order to get about.

But perhaps his strongest need was to try whatever it took to satisfy his unspecified but vicious craving for revenge, whether against fate, able-bodied people, his brothers, anyone more successful than he was, anyone in authority, God – or possibly whoever was responsible for a telegram sent to his mother on the eve of his wedding. This told her that her aunt and two cousins in Poland, whom she had been unable to make contact with despite many months of trying, had been murdered by the Nazis, which made her scream and collapse on to the kitchen floor.

But whoever or whatever it was that lay behind Sam Golub's constant quest for revenge, it would stay with him until his death, which itself would be a cruel parody of what happened to him at the age of twelve.

Ten

In the early post-war years, with both men in their mid-twenties, Benjamin Pomeranski generally developed a more adult perspective on life. But he did so without in any way loosening his protective bond with Samuel Golub, who showed no increase at all in maturity or decrease in pugnacity. And he remained ever able to awaken Benny's proclivity for 'the alternative way', which Sam, somewhat less subtly, relished.

The pair's closeness was demonstrated by a notable incident that took place shortly after Benny was demobilised from the Royal Artillery, where he had reached the rank of bombardier. It was a kind of ritualistic farewell to the East End, both Benny and Sam having arranged to move across the river to Brixton, where a number of Jewish families and individuals had settled, most of them entirely respectable but a small handful less so.

Prominent among the latter was Jack Lewis, the noisy, tough individual known as 'Little' Jack. Benny had come across him during the war when the two of them were part of a group sent to a talk given by a Jewish chaplain in the artillery. And it was Little Jack who fuelled Benny's ambition to seek out post-war opportunities in South London, not all of them lawful.

Little Jack's family had lived in and around Brixton for a couple of generations (Jack himself acquired a large house in Streatham) and he had inherited a furniture business built up from nothing by his father. Within months of his discharge from the army – where he had been commended for bravery during the Italian campaign – 'Little Jack' Lewis already had his fingers in a few, mainly unsavoury, pies. In the process, he had recruited a handful of pliable, amoral and unscrupulous characters who were willing to support him in his determination to make a lot of money without much caring how it was done just as long as they in turn could fill their pockets.

All of this helped Little Jack to become wealthy enough to buy a bomb-damaged meeting hall in Richmond, close to the river just south-west of London, and turn it into a jazz club, which, he said, was his 'labour of love'. He had made pilgrimages to New York and even New Orleans in pursuit of jazz. He played the trumpet himself, though not to a professional standard and certainly well below that of his American idols. And, while his villainous lieutenants patronised and sometimes helped out at the 'Jax' Club, Little Jack himself ensured that the two resident staff members there were kosher and more or less above board.

Little Jack also had links, familial and otherwise, with the East End and was able to find out quite a lot more than he'd known during the war about his young army friend Benny Pomeranski, including his friendship with a 'loose cannon' called Samuel Golub.

'It seems that my old wartime pal is quite the big shot, the *ganzer macher*, in Brixton,' Benny told Sam. 'And he has people in Brick Lane and Bethnal Green. He seems to know all about us. I think we need to show him what we're made of. Make an impression. I don't want to be beholden to him. He's obviously a tough guy but I don't think he's a total brute. Underneath the show of ruthlessness, he's basically a solid Jewish family man – he's got a couple of kids – and he can be very useful, help us find our feet… If you want to soften him up, just talk about jazz – he loves it.'

'Well, you know me well enough, Benny,' said the cocksure young Samuel Golub. 'I ain't scared of anybody, including Brixton's Mr Big. Yeah, let's say our big, bad goodbye to the East End and then, when your Little Jack mate gets to hear about it, he'll be impressed enough to know not to push us around.'

'Okay, then, Sammy boy. See if you can come up with something. Not some cheap robbery – you know how I feel about robbery.'

'Yeah, you're very selective.'

'That's right. But, seriously, Sam, see if you can come up with something stylish, something that doesn't hurt anybody who doesn't deserve to be hurt.'

'There are people who do deserve to get hurt.'

'Of course. But, whatever you come up with, let it be, as you say, something that will impress a few people. But, afterwards, I don't think we should waste too much time worrying about Little Jack Lewis. We were perfectly friendly in the army. He's actually quite funny.'

Sam regarded Little Jack's menacing reputation as a challenge, but he still needed Benny's guidance and counsel of restraint. And, however fearless Sam in particular felt, the two friends would have to tread carefully in their first few weeks in Brixton, especially where Little Jack was concerned. However small his information network was, and however much it relied on the likes of sisters, cousins and aunts, it was clearly efficient. Indeed, it had already been reported to Jack that Sam Golub had 'ideas above his standing' to which Jack retorted, '*standing* is something I hear he can't do very well. Not without a stick, at any rate. And, coming into a different manor, he needs to know not to try to run before he can walk, with or without his walking stick.'

On the day of their 'big, bad goodbye to the East End', Benny and Sam, both with their thick, dark hair preened and shining with lotion from Johnny Korb's barber shop in Whitechapel, targeted a local *mumser* – bastard – named Hughie Cartwright, a severe, unsmiling man of around fifty who ran a grocery shop in Vallance Road. It was said he had a 'mentally defective' daughter locked up in his house, though nobody had ever seen her. It was also said that he had supported the Nazis before and during the war and was one of Oswald Mosley's militant fascist 'blackshirts'.

Mostly, the Jews in the neighbourhood avoided Cartwright's shop but, on that long-to-be-remembered day, the two sleekly groomed young friends, having made sure the place was empty of customers, entered, drew the bolt across the door to lock themselves in, and turned the 'Open' sign to show the word 'Closed' to the street outside.

They then began to torment Hughie Cartwright. They jeered childishly and called him names – *Hughie Cartwright! He can't fart right!* Then they stained his starched white apron with molasses from an open barrel. After that, they broke all the eggs they could find, tipped flour on the counter and generally made a mighty mess.

Sam was particularly keyed up and swept a large jar of treacle off the counter with his walking stick and told Cartwright that, if he should tell on them to anyone, particularly the police, his life – and that of any family he happened to have, 'including any lunatic daughter' – would not be worth the living. (Benny would later chide Sam for drawing too heavily and obviously on the dialogue of gangster films he had seen at the Hackney Pavilion.)

The two young rogues did not realise that there was another man – a supplier – in a back room of the shop. As they began knocking things off the shelves, the supplier stepped out to remonstrate with them. He was a large, corpulent, red-faced man with big, glistening ears, one of which supported a stubby pencil. His eyes bulged and his substantial stomach pushed at the buttons of his striped shirt as he shouted at Sam, who was the nearer to him of the two young intruders: 'Get out of here, you bloody little Yids. You got what was coming to you in the last war. Don't you people ever learn? Don't think you're safe round here, either. Mark my words, pal.'

The way that young Samuel Golub marked the supplier's words was by picking up the treacle jar from the floor and cracking the man across the head with it, dislodging the pencil from behind his ear and sending him to the sawdusted floor.

Sam then gathered up his stick and he and Benny stepped briskly out of the shop, Sam in his distinctive hobbling style. As they unlocked the door, he laughed and restored the sign to 'Open'. Benny, the less audacious of the two, turned it back to 'Closed'.

Eleven

'What's it like working for Monty?'
'Mostly despicable.'

He laughed. Not token, being-sociable laughter but the genuine, unforced kind. Laughter of surprise, relief even. Laughter that was part of the experience of getting closer to this thrilling woman.

'Actually,' she went on, 'I spend a lot of time working with Davy nowadays. He's a sweetheart. Very different to his brother-in-law. Occasionally, when we sit on the piano stool together practising, he puts his arm round me and gives me a little squeeze.'

'*What*? Davy Greenhouse?'

'Yes. He's harmless. A good musician. And kind. Like I said, he's a sweetheart. A greenhouse, not a hothouse.'

Benny knew already, from listening to Estelle Davis's voice, hearing her sing and recognising the depths of emotion she could convey, that she was exceptional. But there was much more. He soon discovered that she was intelligent, witty, funny and strong-willed. It seemed that his eager anticipation, ignited by her mere presence, was being fulfilled.

But she was also forthright: 'Do you love your wife,' she asked, suddenly without warning.

Estelle and Benny were sitting at a corner table in the Astoria café. It was a Wednesday afternoon, half-day closing in Brixton. The shutters at Pomeranski Gowns were pulled down at one o'clock.

Bertha was doing what she often did on Wednesday afternoons – visiting her sister Louise in Waltham Abbey having arranged for the young next-door neighbour Angela to collect Simon from school. None of the other Astorians were in the café, just a few locals enjoying a late steak-and-kidney-pudding-and-two-veg lunch, or stirring and sipping teas and chicory-based 'coffees', biting into scones, Chelsea buns and Bakewell tarts, or just smoking and pressing cigarette butts into overloaded ashtrays.

'Yes,' Benny answered her blunt question immediately. 'I do love her. What about you? Your husband, or ex-husband? Monty – not that you can believe everything he says – told me you were divorced.'

'No. We're not divorced.' She laughed and shook her head. 'Couldn't be bothered. My old man's not worth bothering with. And he's buggered off to America.'

'But I presume you loved him once.'

'Do not presume. Hey, look at that old couple at that table near the door.' She pointed out a rheumy-eyed man with a thin, erratic bush of white hair who was carefully replacing a teacup into its saucer while his wife, a tiny, wrinkled, sparrow-like woman, was inquisitively gazing around the room.

'They're sweet,' Benny said.

'They're *merged*,' Estelle said.

'That's lovely,' he said, misinterpreting her forceful tone. 'That's kind of what I'm thinking about, that kind of love, when I say I love my wife. You build up familiarity over the years. That can only get deeper and, gradually, more intimate. Even if you fight from time to time. You come to understand each other, your personalities, your little ways. Because you've made your nest together – your home. And in the same way that your home becomes a kind of extension of yourself, so does the person you married, and, as you say, you merge.'

Estelle held up her hand. 'It's not lovely,' she said. 'It's not love that you're describing. It's habit. *Merging*, in the way I'm talking about it, is not a good thing because it involves giving up your individuality. Surrendering. I was talking about that just the other day with my friend Ruth. I believe you sat next to her at the Fox. At the opening.'

'Yes, *your* opening. Your brilliant opening. Yeah, Ruth. She seemed full of fun. I wasn't so keen on her boyfriend, though...'

'Did she tell you about the club where she worked before the Fox?'

'No,' Benny shook his head and pressed his lips together.

'Run by a friend of Monty's,' she added.

'What's his name?'

'Can't remember exactly. Monty – and Ruth – only referred to him by his surname. I've forgotten. Conway or Connor or something. Costa? Oh, I can't remember.'

Benny shook his head again: 'Doesn't ring any bells.'

'He sounds a bit like Monty – fat bloke apparently,' said Estelle with a short laugh before going on to make a rare concession in Monty's favour: 'Although, to be fair to Monty, he doesn't expect you to be a prostitute to bring your pay up to a living wage. Unlike Mr Conman or whatever his effing name is.'

Estelle took a breath and then continued: 'Ruth doesn't like to talk about it. She's very secretive. She just says that she felt complete contempt for all of the men. Including some feller she actually married. There's none of that at the Sly Fox. Monty tells the waitresses off if they flirt with the customers, or even laugh.' Another breath, and: 'I can understand why Ruth wants to draw a veil over her past. If I was her, I wouldn't want people thinking that of me. Selling my body.' A pause, and then: 'I wouldn't want *you* thinking that of me.'

'I certainly don't,' Benny hastily reassured her, though he felt a little shocked to hear about Estelle's close friend and working colleague. 'I didn't even think it of Ruth, your friend,' he said. She seemed quite wrapped up with her boyfriend. Mind you...'

She interrupted him: 'They're not talking.'

'What?'

'The old couple at the table by the door. They're not talking. They're not looking at each other. He's looking into the teapot and she's looking at other customers in the café and ignoring him. You got a light?' she asked, pulling a cigarette case out of her handbag.

'Sorry, I'm trying to give up smoking.'

'Oh, here we are, it doesn't matter. I've got a book of matches in my bag after all. Never mind.' And then, having struck a match and lit a cigarette, Estelle continued speaking:

'Yes, I admit, you do sometimes see old couples who love each other. Caring, paying attention. Sharing interests. Laughing, holding hands. But, more often, they're like those two over there. Nothing to say to each other. Much more lonely than if they were actually living on their own. I'd shoot myself.

'We all need to talk to each other, freely, all the time. We are blessed with language. After all those years together, that familiarity you're describing, you'd surely know how to communicate. Even if you're feeling anger, pain or resentment, *talk* about it. Describe it. Get it off your chest. It's a big world and there's lots to do and talk about, and laugh about. Like we're doing. And we've only just met.'

Estelle drew pneumatically on her cigarette as Benny replied. 'You're right. And I agree, there are different ways to merge.' In his imagination, he was already contemplating the possibility of merging the personal history, geography and connectivity that he and Bertha shared – the having of a child, the endearing recognition of each other's quirks, the *comfort* – with the intensity, artistry, newness and excitement, the *danger*, of Estelle. Could that be done? Long odds against.

'Does the sheer *difference* mean that the one can perfectly complement the other, and you can have both, satisfying different needs,' he asked himself later that evening sitting alone at home with a glass of whisky, Bertha not yet having returned from her sister's, 'or that the two kinds of love will repel each other and tear the lover – me – apart? Or is it *predetermined*?' – he laughed but also inwardly congratulated himself at his choice of the word – 'Or a law of science that one will overpower and destroy the other? Warmth against fire. Sentimentality versus sensuality. It doesn't sound like a fair match.'

Although this conversation with himself took place soundlessly in Benny's head, not always even forming into words or phrases, when these did come he enjoyed articulating them audibly, revelling in their quiet but eloquent sound: 'predetermined', 'warmth against fire', 'sentimentality versus sensuality'.

'I suppose,' he silently reflected, 'that it depends not on the experience but upon the experiencer – again, me. Why am I so ridiculously thrilled that she was keen for me not to think she was a whore? A singing whore. Hah! Never entered my head. She made a point of it: "I wouldn't want *you* to think that of me," she said.'

He smiled and took out a record from the sideboard cabinet, an LP of Ella Fitzgerald singing the *Rodgers and Hart Songbook*, and placed it on the gramophone turntable, before lifting the tonearm and bringing the needle down with careful precision at the penultimate track: 'My Heart Stood Still'.

A week later, Benny was relaying these intimate personal reflections to Joseph Pelovsky – Spanish Joe. 'What? Are you mentally casting yourself as a kind of Persian shah,' Joe teased, 'with a miniature harem? Bertha and Estelle? These are two strong-minded women you are talking about.'

Benny laughed and shook his head. 'No, no,' he said. 'I suppose I am imagining two separate relationships at the same time, until real decisions and choices have to be made.' And then, wistfully, with a shrug: 'Oh, I don't know.'

For the first few weeks of secrecy, in which the fast-growing relationship between Estelle and Benny was veiled, Spanish Joe was Benny's trusted confidant, an arrangement cemented by the two men's burgeoning friendship.

Their interests coincided to a large extent across a wide cultural spectrum. Joe was the only Astorian apart from Benny who liked to read serious fiction. He had also had classical piano training as a very young man and his record collection still reflected that. He introduced Ralph Landau to opera. But he shared Benny's love of jazz, too, and, on one sublime summer's evening, he and Ralph, by then his lover, accompanied Benny and Bertha to a concert given by the young American jazz pianist Erroll Garner at the new Royal Festival Hall. They arrived late and, as they climbed the stairs to the auditorium, they could hear the first tune, 'The Way You Look Tonight', coming from speakers in the foyer.

They had to wait for the tune to finish before being admitted to take their seats and so they stood, two couples happily holding hands, looking out through the window on to the Thames gently glinting in the late sunlight. For Benny, Erroll Garner helped not merely to normalise Joe and Ralph's relationship, but to unify all four of them in the pricelessly beautiful moment.

Benny had grown up without any real knowledge or understanding of homosexuality and through his adolescence and early adulthood had indifferently recognised it as a taboo and indeed a crime. The physical idea of it disgusted him, and would always do so. As far as he and his circle were concerned, it was a subject for 'smutty' jokes. And as he became more aware of its prevalence from gossip among his Empress associates about television and stage performers, he felt revolted, and recoiled from any reference to it. Then, when first the multi-talented Ralph Landau and then 'Spanish' Joe Pelovsky came along and easily fitted in with the Astoria boys, he became intrigued and much more sympathetic – and having them as part of the gang fitted into his field of vision, encompassing as it did a gathering-in of the varied and gifted, which was what he believed he was doing.

Benny frequently had his own private conversations with Spanish Joe and both men were nothing if not candid. One of the first such conversations took place at a table at the very edge of the bar area at Jax during a long interval between performances. The two men compared their feelings about, respectively, Estelle and Ralph.

'I have to confess,' said the 'Fixer' to the 'Spanish' sales rep, 'I still cannot understand the idea of physical attraction between two men. Is that how it has always been for you?'

'Oh no. As a teenager, and up to about the age of twenty-one, I went out with girls, quite a lot of them. Plenty of sex, too. I sought after a certain type of beautiful woman. I always went for women who were aware of their good looks and had a very feminine elegance. On several occasions, sometimes desperately, I chased after older women.

'These classy and sometimes snooty females were always very poised and infinitely more confident and adept than I was, especially the older birds. Overcome by what I saw as them condescendingly allowing me to hold and enter their bodies, I came to realise that my frenzied "technique" was actually very aggressive. Certainly not tender or loving. It was definitely not satisfying.

'And I realised that what I was doing was punishing them for what I saw as their cold superiority. Trying to get my own back for feeling inferior; trying fiercely to knock them off their pedestals. There was always a bit of "stuck-up bitch, who does she think she is" business. I was angry, too, I suppose, that none of them seemed to realise how lucky they were to have been born female.

'And then,' Joe continued, taking a long inhalation from the cigarette he was smoking, 'I was sitting in a café one afternoon in Brighton, just after I started my first job with those wedding-dress wholesalers, and in walked Roger, who was to become my first genuine love.'

'And he turned your life around? Brought out the real you?'

Joe nodded in assent. 'He brought out the real me.'

'As it happens,' said Benny softly, 'I'm going to Brighton next weekend, hopefully with somebody who seems to be bringing out the real me.'

Twelve

There was an inevitability about the way Max Baskin – Maxie the Ganoff – turned out. Having grown up in poverty in Spitalfields in the wake of the First World War, he was frequently described in his youth as having 'a chip on his shoulder'.

The youngest and only boy among the five children of two Russian immigrants, Maxie always resented what he saw as his parents' favouring of his four sisters throughout his childhood. He grew much taller and bulkier than the girls yet felt bullied by them. And indeed they were, individually and collectively, prone to taunt him, often on account of his size and his slowness of movement compared to their frenzied and bustling way of going about their daily lives.

At school, too, Maxie felt marginalised. The active intelligence, spontaneity and thought processes of the clever, playful and confident children at the centre of school life were beyond his conceiving. Young Max incarnated Shakespeare's 'whining schoolboy with his satchel'. Maxie's satchel, in addition to books and pencils, contained packages of food that his mother gave him every morning and he carried it heavily along the pavement, additionally weighed down by assumptions of his own inadequacies.

And, again like Shakespeare's whining pupil, he would 'creep like snail unwillingly to school'. But who wouldn't in Maxie's place, faced with the intimidating sights and sounds of the noisy playground and the cruel classroom? But his adolescence, the next of the bard's seven ages of man, did not, as in *As You Like It*'s prognosis, elide uninterruptedly from whining to loving. Although Maxie would in his time indeed 'sigh like furnace' and, at least in his mind, fashion 'woeful ballads', neither his sighs nor his ballads would be addressed directly to any even minimally reciprocating mistress. For none existed.

One day, after school, four or five boys were huddled outside the gates and one of them peeled off from the rest as Maxie was passing. 'Hey, come with us, big feller,' he said, smirking but not in an unfriendly way.

'Where?' Maxie asked.

'We're going on a nickin' spree,' the boy revealed.

Unusually, Maxie allowed curiosity to overcome his normal reticence and he followed his classmates to the Woolworths store in Mare Street, Hackney.

It turned out to be the most exciting experience of his life up that point. Well-planned, too, by the boy who had recruited him, the natural leader (naturally envied by Maxie) of the pack of petty pinchers. They were all to separate at the shop entrance and meet later in London Fields to compare their booty before going on to a nearby café. By then, to his delighted surprise, Maxie's haul from the open counters – of sweets, toys, pencils and other small trifles and oddities – would easily match those of his pilfering companions. As for the store management, 'they are *asking* for it,' Maxie said to himself. And so was born a lifetime of kleptomania.

Although the young Max Baskin rarely stole anything of real value, he thrived on the risk, which in later years resulted in a couple of brief spells in prison – the only one of the Astorians during their heyday to do time (though Benny the Fixer was once fined for receiving a batch of 'dodgy' dresses). This was in deep contrast to the crooks within Little Jack's retinue, notably the twins Tommy and Billy Smith. Following the routine but botched robbery of a garage, Tommy was jailed for the murder of the garage attendant while Billy, having struck out with a shovel at a policeman trying to arrest him on the garage forecourt, was banged up for grievous bodily harm, leaving Jack without both his right-hand man and his driver.

The case that saw the Smith twins sent down took place a week before Sam moved to Brixton, a month before Benny's arrival and two years before the momentous lunch at the smaller of the Astoria cinema café's two rooms, to which Benny and Sam invited Joe Pelovsky (long before a young Simon Pomeranski initiated Joe's 'Spanish' tag), Maxie 'The Ganoff' Baskin, Harry 'Fancy Goods' Miller and professional entertainer Ralph Landau, who was known in show-business circles as a 'versatile violinist' but disparagingly described by Sam as 'queer as a four-pound note' and nicknamed 'Pansy Potter' – the name of a character, 'the strongman's daughter', in the children's comic, the *Beano*.

It didn't take long for Ralph and fashion rep Joe Pelovsky to come together in a way closer than merely being fellow members of the Astorian gang, in which sphere Ralph was very useful in that he could put Benny or Sam in touch with all sorts of underpaid music-hall hoofers, warblers and jokers willing to earn a naughty quid or two. Meanwhile, Joe, the cleverest of the Astorian boys apart from Benny, would bring a dash of flair to the proceedings.

During a get-together in the Astoria café in the Astorians' early days, Joe, after a couple of generous measures of whisky, put his arm around Ralph and declared 'war' on 'normal society'. Pulling Ralph closer to him, the future 'Spanish' Joe decided that this gathering of characters on the margin was the moment and the place to release some of his repressed feelings. 'Society brands me, and people like me,' he declared, smiling at Ralph, 'as criminals, so I might as well live up to the name. I am more than happy to break the rules of our tight-arsed society and get my hands on its plundered profits. For some people, that's socialism, or communism. For me, it's vengeance, pure and simple.'

The Astorian group wasn't deliberately an exclusive male set-up. But, while Bertha Pomeranski, Benny's wife, wanted nothing to do with it, Joyce Golub was firmly told by her husband Sam not to have anything to do with it even if she wanted to. In time, Fancy Goods Harry would quite often bring his mistress, Vera Coleman, to group meetings and, later still, Estelle Davis sat in on a few get-togethers, always with something to say for herself.

Leaving aside the fringe female involvement of Vera and Estelle, the last – and youngest – joiner, in 1953, was Joey Campbell who, having left Little Jack's employment, was taken on trust as an Astorian; it was Sam who named him 'Joey the Boxer', whereas in the ring he became known as Kid Joey. He never said much at the Astoria gatherings but liked being there and sometimes helped out with strong-arm stuff.

For a few weeks, Benny and the others remained circumspect as far as Joey was concerned because his connections with Little Jack had not been entirely severed. In any event, he was at that time preoccupied with his boxing career and saw more of his manager than of any other individual, including any of his string of girlfriends.

Meetings were arranged ad hoc, or arose from a spontaneous get-together in the café of two or three of the Astorian group, and were completely informal. There would usually be an agenda but nothing was formally written down except times, locations and other details of specific jobs or, as Benny liked to call them, 'operations'. The café's owner, Luigi Mantella, was always happy to let the Astorians meet, even at short notice, in the smaller of its two rooms, with its doors closed, and sometimes locked, for privacy – and he was well paid for doing so.

In setting up the Astorians, however informally, Benny Pomeranski felt very pleased with himself, pleased that he had accomplished something that, in his eyes, was worth accomplishing. Despite their various robberies and assaults, purportedly always and only directed at those 'who deserved it' – bullies, 'real' thieves, 'nasty' bosses, greedy companies, sexual exploiters, unreconstructed fascists – Benny never thought of the Astorians as a criminal ring.

Rather, he believed he had built a *team*, variously and collectively imaginative, fearless and committed to putting the world to rights, not doing wrong. He was especially pleased to have created something beyond a bunch of fairly conventional male Jewish shopkeepers who had managed to drag themselves out of the poverty and poor education in which they were brought up – a team that, over the years of its existence, smoothly integrated a lame but dangerous individual, a young black man, a couple of occasional women – and two homosexual men. And as for the trio of Jewish shopkeepers among them, not one of them was at all conventional.

Benny liked to think that all aspects of his life were connected and somehow consistent with each other. That the books he read and the music he listened to flowed from the same source that nourished his activities outside the law – and that these were all of a piece with his legit *gesheft*, Pomeranski Gowns, and could be fitted into the same moral framework.

Certainly, some of the Astorian boys could, in their younger days, be a bit wild, and would brazenly tell you they would 'take no nonsense' from anybody (Sam continued to display this attitude until his last days) but generally they didn't provide the lawyers with too much overtime. Their single most audacious criminal collaboration actually lived up to that old gangland hyperbole about being 'undetectable'.

It also, in keeping with the times, rode roughshod over minority sensibilities. For this so-called (by Benny) 'unimaginable heist' involved the exploitation of both an unfortunate *faygeleh*, (or, in broader slang, 'poof') and, without any acknowledgement by the Astorians of tribal brotherhood, 'a bunch of *frummers*' (seriously religious Orthodox Jews).

One October evening in 1954, a clutch of Astorians were seated around the big table in the Astoria café's private room to celebrate Fancy Goods Harry's birthday. Luigi had brought out a clean white tablecloth and placed two carafes of his best Chianti Rosso in the centre. Everyone present was in good spirits and, after passing round a carafe for all present to fill their glasses, Spanish Joe held up his drink and called for a toast: 'Here's to Harry, our very own fancy man. May he have a lovely birthday and many happy returns.'

Fancy Goods Harry stayed in his seat while the others – Benny, Spanish Joe, Maxie the Ganoff and Vera – stood and sang a chorus of 'Happy Birthday' before breaking into boisterous laughter.

As Spanish Joe raised his glass, Benny noticed a sparkling new diamond ring on the third finger of his left hand. 'That's really sharp, Joe,' said Benny, pointing at the ring, 'and it looks expensive.'

'It *is* expensive,' Spanish Joe confirmed. 'Or at least it would be if you were to buy it in a jeweller's shop. Bloody expensive. I'm glad you noticed it. Ralph gave it to me yesterday just before he left for Australia.' Ralph Landau had been booked for a six-week season as part of a music-hall company touring Australian cities, beginning in Melbourne. With a range of skills that extended to juggling, sword-swallowing and fire-eating, he was much in demand.

'Well, that kind of rock is not exactly difficult to notice,' said Benny, his eyes trained on Spanish Joe's left hand.

'I know,' said Spanish Joe. 'I was going to raise the subject here, if Fancy Goods doesn't mind. I think there's an operation we could work in connection with it.'

'We're all ears, I'm sure. Sorry, Harry, we'll get on to some more birthday stuff later. But you look comfortable enough for the time being.'

This last remark of Benny's triggered a general laugh, in view of the fact that Vera was now sitting on Harry's lap. 'Spanish Joe,' said Benny with a theatrical sweep of his hand, 'the floor is yours.'

'Well,' Spanish Joe began by waving his ringed finger around for all to see, 'Ralph got me this wonderful ring through this old flame of his. A religious feller, works in Hatton Garden. Or Farringdon, to be precise.'

'Oh,' Fancy Goods Harry chipped in, 'I imagine that, being a fire-eater, Pansy P – sorry, *Ralph* – must have lots of old flames.'

Spanish Joe couldn't help smiling along with the burst of laughter that greeted Fancy Goods's comment. 'I'll let you off,' Spanish said to Harry, 'because it's your birthday.' The Chianti was already beginning to take effect.

'Is it the real McCoy?' Maxie asked.

'Oh it's the real McCoy, all right,' Spanish said proudly. 'Worth a few hundred that ring is. Ralph picked it up for seventy-five.'

A faint whistling sound issued from Benny's lips as he blew out his cheeks. 'Hey, Fancy Goods, birthday boy,' he said, addressing a man who was knowledgeable about costume jewellery and therefore the nearest thing to an expert in the room. 'You know about these things, Harry. Put Vera down a minute and have a butcher's at that diamond. Would you mind showing it to him, Joe?'

Fancy Goods Harry produced a jeweller's eyeglass from his inside pocket and Spanish Joe took off the ring and surrendered it to Harry's scrutiny. 'Yeah, that's a good rock,' said Harry, having screwed the glass into his eyesocket. 'Way out of my league, though.'

'Really,' said Benny, and, turning to Spanish Joe, asked, 'How come Ralph got it so cheap? Knocked off, was it?'

'No, that's the thing,' Spanish said. 'It's not knocked off. There's a renegade bunch of gem dealers who have this secure warehouse, a distribution point off Farringdon Road for imported goods that originated in Africa and on the Continent. Every accredited dealer has a strongbox, a key and a code. Ralph's contact even hinted that some accredited dealer's names are invented. They never existed. Or they died years ago.

'Once a month, after the stuff is sorted out between the dealers in this particular warehouse, they get together to trade off anything that's made its way in above the official shipment tallies. A form of smuggling. Sometimes there's not much, but in a good month there can be loads. They sell to each other, or occasionally to more kosher dealers in the market, at knockdown prices – you know, for their personal use, their families and so on. Thousands of pounds' worth can get shifted for discounts of up to ninety per cent, or they just exchange some stuff among themselves. They're dealers – they do deals. They have to shift it, see. It's surplus stock. And not exactly lawfully acquired.'

'Interesting,' said Benny, nodding.

'I'd love to get my hands on some of that stuff,' said Maxie.

'I need to talk to a man about this,' Benny said, stroking his moustache.

'Which man?' asked Vera, her eyes widening.

'The Stick,' Benny replied. 'We've got to keep this within our confines. Joe, make sure you don't wave that rock around anywhere near Little Jack or his zombies.'

'Amen,' said Maxie, nodding slowly.

Thirteen

'A perfect fit.'

'Yes, yes. We are. This is a made-to-measure love affair.'

'"Made to measure". That's nice. Your father must have been a tailor.'

'No, my old man *pressed* suits and trousers. He didn't make them.'

'That doesn't sound so romantic. I prefer pressing bodies to pressing clothes – especially *our* two bodies.'

After their exploratory tea in the Astoria café earlier in the week, Benny had asked Estelle to lunch the next day, out of town this time, in Harrow, as he was 'travelling' – driving, as he now and then did, to a range of suppliers and factories on the outskirts of London – and an expensive bottle of wine had helped to stimulate their senses. 'I've got someone to see in Brighton over the weekend,' he told her. 'Why don't you come with me?'

'What about Bertha?'

'She's practically living with her semi-invalid sister at the moment.'

'Yes please, I'll come,' she'd said in a prompt, decisive manner. 'I know I should feel guilty but I don't. Quite the opposite. I feel a buzz of excitement…' And, on parting, it was impossible to say who had initiated it but the sudden, searching kiss they shared felt completely right.

And now they were in Brighton, on the first day after their first night in a luxury double room Benny had booked at the Grand

Hotel on the seafront, having breezed in on a Friday evening, no questions asked.

'I loved it that you read poetry to me this morning,' she said, with no care for the breakfast they were about to miss. 'Who'd've thought it?'

'I didn't read it very well. I wanted to say it to you off by heart but I wasn't sure I could learn it in time even though it's one of the most famous poems of all time.'

'It must be one of the most beautiful poems of all time. I just love being compared to a summer's day.'

'*More lovely and more temperate,*' he said, and kissed her forehead and then her mouth, the kiss deepening and propelling them across the sheet in horizontal passion. And, when they stopped to draw breath, she held his body tight, her eyes now looking over his back and shoulder towards the window and the sea beyond.

'We have a lovely summer's day of our own,' she said. 'We should get up and sample the sea air.'

'No, not yet. It will shorten the joy and increase the sadness of the moment.'

'Sadness?'

'I know it sounds mad but the complete joy I feel in your arms also makes me sad because I know it's not forever. Every beginning brings with it an end. That's the pity of life. The stronger the happiness, the sadder I feel knowing that it can only be temporary. It can't last.'

'I feel so different to you. For me, it's a beginning. An exciting beginning. I can't think about the end. I'm finding out more about you all the time. The way you talk, it's so lovely. So enthusiastic. So clever.'

'It depends on who I'm speaking to. You managed to unlock feelings that were locked so deeply inside me. You've drawn out my romantic side. Before you came along, this thing that we have, I experienced only as theory. A very slow-burning, generalised desire, like a boy, not yet a man.'

'But reading me poetry! That's never happened to me before. And how's that come about? You're an East End boy who left school at fourteen or fifteen. You should have had a proper education.'

'Ah, I did better than that. I had an improper one. On the streets. But I loved going to the library, and also at home my mum always encouraged me to read. We didn't go that often to the synagogue but my dad sometimes on Sunday nights sat with us three boys and got us to read bits from the Bible and the prayer book. "Isn't that beautiful?" he would say. "Isn't that beautiful?" My brother Cyril and I used to mimic him – *"Isn't that beautiful"* – but only behind his back. We wouldn't dare do it to his face.'

'But who did you read poetry with? Do you read to Bertha?'

'I used to, quite a lot.'

'But with your friends? I can't see Sam the Stick discussing Shakespeare.'

'Ah, that's a different kind of attachment. We grew up together. And I was with him when he had his horrific accident. I thought he was going to die. And, at first, they were going to take his leg off, or at least part of it. He was a truly wild boy but he didn't deserve the deal he was handed.

'But of course we are very different,' Benny continued, voicing the distinction he had always been aware of. 'I doubt that Sam has read a book in his entire life whereas I've always loved reading. Since I was a kid. Reading on my own in a quiet room. I don't get much chance to do that these days.'

'Since you met me, you mean…'

'*Mmm*,' he smiled and hugged her affectionately.

'But,' he sat up and continued, 'Spanish Joe and I – and Harvey from the record shop in Excelsior Arcade, and Henry Kenton the tailor – often talk about books. And music, which I intend to do with you, my darling.'

'Kiss me,' she said, looking into his eyes. And, revelling in their nakedness, they locked together into a kiss that was never going to remain just a kiss.

'I can't believe this is happening,' he said to her.

'It very much is,' she said, wrapping her legs around his, bringing on the mutually desired response...

'Cigarette?' Estelle's clicking open of her cigarette case, as she picked it up from her bedside table, was, apart from their satisfied breathing, the first sound or movement either of them made having laid their heads back on their respective pillows in a post-climactic stillness. 'No thanks,' he said. 'I've given them up.'

Estelle struck a match and held its flame to the cigarette between her lips, sucking in the tobacco's quick charge and aroma and then exhaling from deep below her chest. With her eyes focused on the ceiling, she said, 'Can you remember what first attracted you to me?'

'You have a perfect bum.'

'I'd rather be told that I have an intelligent face.'

'That was just a joke. I just said the first silly thing that came to mind,' Benny said, turning his smile into a brief, closed-mouth laugh. 'From where I was sitting when I first saw you at the Sly Fox, I couldn't even see your bum. No, it was your mouth. Not only is your mouth sexy, but it is the part of you through which your beautiful voice emerges. But what is really wonderful about your singing is that it projects the whole of you. So, while it might have been your mouth, your lips, that first caught my eye, it was immediately the whole of you that had me hooked.'

'Oh, *darling*. You are so romantic. Honestly,' Estelle said, exhaling again, not quite as deeply as before. 'Tell me, do they really call you the fixer?'

'Sometimes.'

'Well, you've certainly fixed me,' she said. To which Benny's smile took on a self-satisfied expression.

'I feel we have a special connection,' he said to her later as they walked along the esplanade and down on to the stony beach, breathing in the sea's confection of fragrances.

'Or are we just mad about each other,' she said, adjusting her sunglasses to lessen the powerful brightness. 'Or are we just mad, full stop? It's an everyday occurrence.'

'No,' he said, 'I believe our coming together is more than physical.'

'But it is pretty damn physical, Benny darling. To which I say hallelujah. And, as the man wrote, and the other man sang: *It had to be you* – and especially for you, Benny Pom-Pom – *And even be glad just to be sad, thinking of you...*'

'Sing it to me, Estebelle, in the car. And then sing some more, later in the hotel room, to give us an appetite before we go out to sample Brighton's best cuisine.'

'Not before you've told me more about our "special connection",' she demanded as she watched a father run into the sea with his two young children, one holding his left hand, the other his right.

'Give me a bit of time. It's not easy to describe but it's very strong,' he said, smiling almost boyishly. 'Wait until I've had time to collect my thoughts.'

At the end of the afternoon, as the sun was cooling and the light was flowing away over the sea, she walked along the shoreline while he was buying a couple of beers from a beachside bar. Most of the trippers had gone or were making their way back to the promenade, some towards the station, others crossing the road to head back for tea and supper in their homes, hotels and boarding houses.

He stopped, holding the glasses of beer in his hands, and stood looking at her from a distance, as if for the first time. She was in a primrose-coloured summer dress he'd bought for her with the bottom of it tucked into her knickers, which from where he stood made her look like a little girl. She was holding her shoes and walking very slowly with her feet just touching the very edge of the water. And, though he couldn't hear her, he knew she was singing quietly to herself. It was a habit of hers.

And then she saw him, standing still beyond the pebbles. She waved and increased her pace, signalling for him to sit down at one of the empty tables in front of the bar, which he did and where, once she joined him, he responded to her continued entreaties to describe their special connection.

'Well,' he said. 'I believe the physical and the mental, the emotional, are a blend and, because it is temporary, I want to seal our beautiful, loving moments into my memory. To make them last. Make them as permanent as is possible. Everything combines in each of those moments – your lovely voice, your skin, your smell, our laughter, our likes and dislikes, our love of the same things, the closeness of you to me. It's like swimming in a tropical ocean.' And he took a sip from his glass. Beer had never tasted better.

'Brighton is not quite tropical,' she said, with a laugh, bringing him down to earth. And then: 'You're hung up on that "temporary" thing, aren't you?'

'Yeah, I am I suppose. Maybe I think I don't deserve such pleasure.'

'You do so deserve it. Most people probably think you are just a rough, tough guy, leader of the Astorians. But you are really so gentle. Poetic, for God's sake. What on earth are you doing selling *shmutters* in Brixton Market?'

'I love it, and I make enough money to buy what I want, work when I want, relax when I want, and be able to listen to voices like Ella Fitzgerald's, Sinatra's – and yours. And…' He stopped speaking, put down his glass, breathed in, closed his eyes and dropped his head to his chest, as though he was reaching inside himself, seeking his soul.

Fourteen

'Let's find this Jewish nancy boy, this *faygeleh*.'

Such was Sam's immediate response when Benny told him about Ralph Landau's religious ex-boyfriend having got hold of a fancy diamond ring at a very low price.

And find him they did. It took a little leaning on Ralph at long-distance but not much – Moishe, the old flame, belonged to the past and meant nothing to him any more. Besides, Ralph was over ten thousand miles away happily preparing for a long, rewarding season on stage.

Moishe – the 'Hatton Garden *faygeleh*', in Sam's less than complimentary description – was a plumpish young man with black hat and coat, beard, ringlets, the full Chasidic deal. And it was Sam who, in his own insistent way, persuaded him to come to the back room of Benny's dress shop one Sunday afternoon when it was closed and give to Benny, Maxie, and Sam himself, all the details of the next 'clearance sale'.

Moishe was reluctant at first but his tongue was loosened when Sam threatened to tell his family about his *faygeleh* ways with young boys – and assured him the whole thing, the raid and all, would be kept totally secret since, if it weren't, the fat little *frummer* would find his ability to locate Arab boys on his trips to the Holy Land severely curtailed.

So it was that, a couple of weeks later, Benny, Sam, Harry,

Maxie and Moishe the bearded *faygeleh*, arrived on the due hour at the warehouse in an alley off the Farringdon Road. Fancy Goods waited outside in his big Humber Super Snipe keeping watch while the others entered the building armed not only with a key, code and password, but also with a weapon or two. Spanish Joe stayed at home on the off chance that Moishe might have recognised him from some 'nancy boy' club or event.

Once the quartet seeking access to the 'sorting room' had negotiated the first few automatic barriers, they found themselves outside a grille gate with a *frummer* operating it from the inside. The *frummer* immediately recognised the *faygeleh*. 'Moish,' he exclaimed through the grille, '*Sholom Aleichem*. Who are your friends?'

'*Aleichem Sholom*,' Moish replied. 'It's okay. They're *mishpocheh* – cousins, who do a little dealing.'

'Okay,' said the gateman, but dubiously. And, eyeing Sam and Benny with undisguised suspicion, said, 'I'll phone through and tell Shimon to prepare for an ID check.'

'I suggest,' said Sam, leaning his face against the bars of the grille, 'that you don't touch that phone, and that you open this gate without any more chat.'

The gateman's indignant retort stuck in his throat when he looked down to see that the object with which he was being prodded through the grille was a pistol. With a baffled, horrified look at Moishe, he raised the gate and, with the gun jabbing his spine, led the little party into a room at the end of a corridor.

Inside, around a dozen, mostly bearded men in big black hats and skullcaps, some wearing frock-coats, were inspecting several piles of assorted gems and other small items of jewellery laid out on a pair of tables. Several were using jewellers' glasses of the kind through which Fancy Goods Harry had first looked at Spanish Joe's ring.

Sam the Stick pointed the gun and motioned with his stick for the men to sit on the floor in a corner of the room, the gateman included. He told them to remove their *shtreimels* – hats – but allowed them to keep on their *kuppels* – skullcaps. Next, he ordered them to place their hands on their heads. 'Okay, nobody will get hurt if we all act sensibly here,' said Sam. They all stayed silent as Maxie produced half-a-dozen sacks and, with Benny, tipped into them all of the items on both tables.

'Right,' announced Sam once Maxie and Benny had finished, 'I want you all to stay here for another hour and then go home, forget about it, and we'll all live happily ever after. Come on, Moish, you come with us.' Moishe followed reluctantly, his hands placed on his head in an attempt to show his associates that he was as much a victim as they were.

At the exit, they were met by Fancy Goods Harry, who had stationed himself outside – 'checking, in the event of any latecomers needing deterring,' as he put it. 'Fortunately, there were none,' he said and marched smartly around the corner to bring the car to the front of the building where Benny the Fixer and Maxie the Ganoff dropped their filled bags into the Humber's capacious boot. Maxie then steered Moishe, his hands no longer on his head, into the front passenger seat and jumped into the back, next to where Sam and Benny had already positioned themselves.

Harry drove north towards Clapton, where Moishe lived, and dropped him off on the high road. Sam then leaned out of the window and ostentatiously blew Moishe a kiss. The young religious man felt fearful and shamed and averted his eyes. But, as the car continued northwards, he could still hear Sam laughing.

Once they were well out of Moishe's sight, Benny signalled to Harry to change direction and head south towards the cottage that Maxie had recently acquired in Kent, where the stuff would be stored until Benny finalised arrangements with a relative in the Caribbean who could unload and pass on the stuff for a very decent price. There was a general sense among the car's passengers of a mission successfully accomplished, but Maxie, who was now sweating, was a little scared. 'Aren't you worried that they saw our faces,' he asked Sam, 'and you with your stick? We'll easily be identified.'

'No, I promise you there is no need to worry.' Sam was as ice-cool as ever. 'If these fellers think Moish – one of their own – is involved, they are certainly not going to the cops. And if I were them, I would think that fat little shirt-lifter was in it up to his overactive *schlong*. And, anyway, these blokes haven't lost a thing. They will just put it down to experience and expenses. They won't want to go public on this nice little number they've got going there. Take it from me. We're home and dry.'

'And,' added Benny, 'that job was a definite one-off. Even though they happen to be a bunch of rascals and doing very nicely, thank you, I am a little uneasy about taking from Jews. And also, it doesn't pay to be seen hanging around the Farringdon Road or Hatton Garden area more than once.'

To celebrate the Farringdon Road job, Benny arranged for a 'boys only' weekend in a smart hotel near the coast at Bournemouth with a lot of eating, drinking and uninhibited celebrations. The wives and girlfriends weren't to be given any details about the Farringdon operation, at least not for the time being, and, Benny the Fixer decided, everyone had earned a little holiday where, together, they could enjoy their triumph.

After Benny's relative had taken care of things at his end and the cash had been shared out, each of the Astorian boys found himself around 'a couple of grand' richer. The most spectacular unloading of this 'bunce' was by Spanish Joe – who bought himself a ticket to Australia to join Ralph – and Sam the Stick, who poured a barrow-load of cash into the purchase of a 'shiny new motor', a Rover specially adapted for his disability. Maxie, by contrast, used most of his share to furnish his recently leased cottage in a sleepy village in Kent.

Sam's car, as it transpired, was a kind of compensation. Knowing he was coming into money, he had allowed Joyce, his wife, to have the house redecorated, which was something she had wanted to do for years. She knew of a good painter and decorator, she said, who would do it cheaply and, even though Sam told her not to worry about the cost, she got this man to do the job. He was a highly talkative Italian who grated on Sam's nerves. He started a couple of days before the Bournemouth weekend and, on Friday, when Sam drove off to the south coast in his brand-new car, he was pleased to get away from the mess and the 'eyetie's' incessant 'jawing'.

When Sam returned home on Sunday night, the house was in darkness. It felt cold when he walked in and switched on the light. On the kitchen table was a letter inside an envelope with his name on it. In the letter, Joyce explained that their marriage was over and that she had left him. She had wanted to many times before, she wrote, but had stayed because she was frightened and had nowhere to go. 'But lately things have got worse and I am tired of you trying to act like a big shot. Take it from me, Samuel, you are no big shot. You are a cheap little villain.'

It was only then, as he put the letter back in the envelope and sank into a chair, that Sam noticed that the decorating had come to a full stop as well.

Fifteen

Although the level of mutual respect between the Astorians and Little Jack's mob was generally low, they were not, in essence, rivals. These were not two gangs locked into a dispute over territory. Brixton may have been their patch but it was exclusively the location of their domestic, social and 'legit' working life – certainly as far as Benny and his crew were concerned.

Each of the Astorians and most of Little Jack's gang, apart from the mercenaries and drifters – and Jack himself – identified strongly with Brixton. Virtually all of the illicit 'jobs' and 'operations' carried out by both of Brixton's recalcitrant teams took place well outside the local SW2 and SW9 postcodes, which, in combination, served as a secure base. For many, Brixton was home.

But Little Jack relished being situated apart, however slightly, from the Electric Avenue/Atlantic Road/Coldharbour Lane hub in which the Astorians were clustered. Even though his centre of operations was within shouting distance, he adopted a superior stance towards them. 'I've never even seen a single film at the Astoria,' he would boast as a way of deprecating Benny and his fraternity's foundation stone.

Little Jack's large family house at Streatham Common was three miles outside Brixton – enough to achieve his desired goal of separation. And he spent as much time as he could on or near the river at Richmond inside or outside his jazz club.

Yet he loved his Acre Lane furniture business, 'Lewis and Son', redolent as it was of his late father. Since the retirement and then death of 'Old Man Lewis' a few years before the Astorians arrived in Brixton, it had become Little Jack's personal stage, where he could perform as outlandishly as he wished.

In the summer, shirtless, wearing a string vest and smoking a cigar, he would bring a table and chairs from the store on to the pavement, sit in the sun and loudly invite passers-by – occasionally using a megaphone – to 'venture inside and see our barmy bargains'. He was even known on the odd occasion to play his trumpet to attract customers. On warm Saturdays, the pavement outside his store would often be clogged with people curious to see what all the noise and bustle was about.

Benny the Fixer, too, went about his business in flamboyant fashion. He charmed and flattered women who emerged from the 'changing room' looking dubious about the dress they were trying on. 'You look fabulous, darling,' Benny would say, with apparent sincerity. Or 'that is absolutely your colour. The dress looks as if it was made for you.'

Benny liked to think of himself and his associates as a kind of Robin-Hood-and-his-merry-men team, robbing or disrupting those who could afford the loss – the rich, the arrogant, the authorities. He was good at threatening violence, and generally avoiding it. When it did come into play, Benny liked to ensure – or perhaps simply tell himself – that it was solely to achieve justice.

And, in those circumstances, it gave him a warm sense of satisfaction, such as it did on the day after Maxie the Ganoff had been roughed up in the street by a high-spirited bunch of 'Teddy boys' – young men who, fired up by the new American rock'n'roll music, dressed up their hooliganism in the old clothes of Edwardian dandies, set off by extravagant hairstyles.

On that day, in the afternoon, the physically and emotionally bruised *Ganoff* recognised the three 'Teds' who had assaulted him the previous day. He happened to see them enter a small terraced house no more than twenty yards from Joey's flat. Which was where Maxie himself was heading – as, separately, were Fancy Goods Harry, Sam the Stick and 'Fiery' Freddie Clarke, a fighter from the gym where Joey trained. And, once they were all gathered in Joey's front room to raise a toast to the young boxer on what was his twenty-fourth birthday, Maxie told the others about his unfortunate experience the previous day and the remarkable coincidence of seeing his attackers on his way to Joey's flat.

About twenty minutes later, Joey the Boxer knocked on his noisy neighbours' door. With such whooping, laughing and shouting going on inside, it took three hefty knocks to bring to the door a tall young man of eighteen or nineteen dressed in a crude abbreviation of an Edwardian suit, with his two grinning comrades standing a couple of feet behind him.

'Excuse me,' Joey said. 'I live just a few doors away,' and he pointed in the direction of his flat. 'I've taken delivery of a big stone statue. It took three blokes plus me to lift it out of the van and into my place. But they're not here today and I've got to get the statue into my back garden. You boys look pretty strong. Would you mind helping me?'

'Yeah, sure, mate,' said the young man who had answered his front door. 'But, I warn you, I charge by the minute. And I'm bloody expensive.' His two friends laughed loudly at this and began horsing around as they followed Joey the short distance to his flat. When they arrived at the open street door and were ushered by Joey into his front room they were surprised to see Sam sitting in an armchair, his hands cupped around the top of his stick. The leading young Ted greeted him with: 'You all right, mate? Sitting it out while we do our strong-men stuff, eh?'

At that moment, Joey came back into the room just in time to deter Sam from making a belligerent response. 'It's just through here,' Joey announced and told the strutting lads to follow him into another room in the centre of the house.

If the trio of Teddy Boys had been surprised to see Sam, they were seriously brought up short at the sight of a welcoming party of Harry Miller, Freddie Clarke and, alarmingly, a bruised Max Baskin, along with Joey Campbell himself. As for Sam Golub, he was, prior to joining the others, bolting Joey's front door to prevent escape.

At that point in their lives, these young toughs found they could create a good time out of everything, frequently at the expense of others. They laughed a lot at the individuals and adult networks around them. They were bent on joyfully overturning established values. They had approached Joey's home, and the bogus task he had asked them to perform, in a collective and customary attitude of scornful enjoyment, sustained by riotous, youthful energy. Unfortunately, however, they had found themselves, in their terms, in the wrong place, at the wrong time, facing the wrong people.

Bertha Pomeranski frequently questioned Benny's rigid notion of justice and did so on that occasion: 'This was not justice,' she told her husband. 'It was disproportionate,' she said, giving deliberate emphasis to the last word. 'That young lad had to crawl back to his home along the pavement on his hands and knees.' She had garnered that particular detail from Maxie the Ganoff himself.

'That "young lad", the night before, had tweaked Maxie's nose, spat at him and kicked his backside,' Benny retorted.

'None of that was anywhere as bad,' Bertha said forcefully, 'as the beating that Joey, Sam and friends dished out to those boys – a handful of kids, immature and highly strung, but kids.'

'Well, those kids will now, I can assure you, be a little more mature. They'll think twice before assaulting a helpless fat old feller. No, Bertha, this was a case of justice being very definitely and effectively done,' Benny argued with a commitment as firm as his wife's.

Little Jack, by contrast, had no such worries over the niceties of justice. Unlike the Pomeranskis, Jack Lewis didn't care who stood in his way in his pursuit of loot. Anyone who did so was an enemy, as far as he was concerned. And Little Jack Lewis was a man who needed enemies. Enemies against whom he could decide when and how to strike.

As a gritty and resolute soldier during the war, admired by his comrades and senior officers alike, he nonetheless envied and resented the politicians and the generals who were able to decide which targets to attack and how to conduct operations. He, Jack Lewis, wanted, in every area of his life, to be in control.

He resented not only the Astorians' having established a place within Brixton's twilight sphere but also Benny Pomeranski's own, individual independence – which Jack was not perceptive enough to realise was merely a cover bolstered by Benny's outwardly calm manner. Inside, he was as dependent as the next man.

The two men maintained a distantly polite social connection, though it fell well short of trust. And Benny did occasionally like to relax at Little Jack's jazz club, sometimes with Sam or Spanish Joe and sometimes on his own (but never with Bertha, whose dislike of jazz was stoked by Little Jack's being a purveyor of it).

One bright July day, when Benny had gone to the club to listen to an American saxophonist of resounding repute, and he and Little Jack were seated outside during the interval talking together 'in a tobacco trance', Jack mused over 'how often the right person gets promoted to the right rank, or job, at the right time. Not very, I'd say.'

'Sometimes a person finds the right place all by himself,' said Benny the Fixer. 'No need for a leg-up from someone else. Jockeying for promotion can be a waste of effort. And you can't alter the world just to suit you.' But Jack was no longer listening.

Although he and his family had long left behind their days of poverty in the East End, Little Jack still felt that fate had placed him beneath his merited level. And, despite his ingrained villainy, he thought of himself as a beneficent human being. He had provided for his family in a large, comfortable home. He donated to charity. At Jax, in Richmond's green and pleasant land, he offered the public the tonic that he believed jazz to be.

He also held out a helping hand to needy individuals of his acquaintance (many of them of questionable character) by dispensing finance, crates of booze, or 'worldly wisdom' to those who – usually as a result of overspending on 'little luxuries' – were struggling to make ends meet (though Jack almost always demanded something back from them, thereby upholding his milieu's culture of constantly owing or being owed). Little Jack believed that, if more people would only listen to him, the world would be a far better, richer place – certainly for Little Jack Lewis. And he had no time at all for anybody who disagreed with him. He believed that whatever was good for himself was thereby good for everybody.

Sixteen

An important feature of Little Jack's somewhat devious social life were the monthly 'whisky evenings' that he held in the large back room of his furniture store for his criminal lieutenants, friends, associates and two or three 'out-of-towners' – criminal gang bosses from the East End, Waterloo, Walworth, Battersea, Soho or elsewhere. Benny and the other Astorians were always invited to these gatherings in what Little Jack called a 'neighbourly' gesture. He even included Joey the Boxer, always letting it be known how magnanimous this was on his part, given that Jack regarded Joey's attachment to Benny's friends and family as 'ungrateful, and just a little bit treacherous – after all, I treated him like a son.'

Behind the hospitality and bonhomie, Little Jack primarily wanted to make sure that every significant villain in South London, and one or two beyond, remained within his purview. The whisky evenings were occasionally awkward or tense but the booze and cigar smoke flowed freely, animosities were mostly kept at bay and the atmosphere was always lively and quite often fun.

Having stocked up with a few bottles of his favourite Scotch whisky (and sometimes the odd Irish or even American Bourbon or Rye whiskey), with the help of a couple of others, Little Jack would drag a large dining table from the display in the shop and carry it into the back room, which was not visible from the street. He would then cover the table with an old tablecloth so that bottles and glasses, and maybe some playing cards, could be placed on it along with food set out by Jack's wife Renée – an array of fish-balls, smoked salmon, cream cheese, potato salad, green salad and various smaller offerings such as olives or salted peanuts.

Earlier in the day, Jack would have gone to Newman's bakery and delicatessen in Coldharbour Lane to buy rye bread, bagels (pronounced 'bygalls' by everyone around that particular table), both pickled and *schmaltz* herring, pickled cucumber, Danish pastries, custard tarts and apple strudel.

Jack's wife Renée sometimes delivered her own culinary creations. On one such occasion, a dark evening with a strong, cold wind blowing outside, she presented a cake she had baked to mark Sam the Stick's birthday, which was coming up later in the week. 'Nice surprise, eh, Sammy,' Jack boomed out. 'Many happy returns. And I'm sure I speak for everybody,' he said, gazing around at the dozen or so people in the room, 'in wishing for the best return of all – Joyce coming back one of these fine days.'

Sam's voice said 'Thank you, Jack' but his eyes said something different, something between 'stop reminding me I am a deserted husband, you loudmouth' and 'what do you care?'

'Thanks, doll,' said Jack to Renée. 'Great spread.'

'And what a "great spread" of truly villainous faces,' Renée said, smiling and lighting a cigarette from a gold-plated cigarette case. 'A choice selection of bad-boy kissers.' Sitting at the corner nearest to where she was standing, Spanish Joe laughed appreciatively. Next to him, Sam the Stick's face was frozen with hard feelings.

'I'll see you out,' Little Jack said to his wife, noisily getting up from the table. Turning back to the room as she and Jack went out, Renée allowed a near-perfect smoke ring to exit her mouth and called out, 'Have a good time, everybody. Happy birthday, Sam.'

As Jack and Renée passed through the shop, the door to the toilet behind the display area opened and a tall blonde woman emerged and smiled nervously at the couple heading towards the street.

'Who's this?' Renée's tone was mischievous, provocative.

'Oh, this is Vera,' Jack explained. 'Vera, this is my wife, Renée.'

'Pleased to meet you,' the two women responded in unison before stepping in opposite directions: Renée outside to Acre Lane and then to the right, across the adjacent Brixton road to the taxi rank at Brixton Oval; Vera inside into an entirely masculine, noisy and smoky cauldron of a room. 'Vera's a friend of Harry's,' Jack said, quietly for once, as he escorted Renée out of the shop. Renée, not so quietly, inquired: 'Is she one of Harry's fancy goods?' and laughed loudly at her own joke.

Back at the table, after downing a couple of glasses of The Famous Grouse, Jack abruptly called the assembled company to order: 'Listen everyone,' he shouted, keen to get the party going. 'Quiet! I've been thinking and I want to ask you all a question. It's been on my mind for a while.' At which point, he grinned salaciously. 'Listen. If you came home and found your missis in bed with another feller...' This brought on an 'Oh I say!' shriek from Vera, rocking back momentarily from Harry. 'Oh, I forgot we had a lady present,' Jack said archly, masquerading as a gentleman. 'Maybe I won't say what I was going to say.'

'Don't worry about me,' said Vera. 'I'll just sit nibbling at this lovely cake. And I'm dying to hear what Harry has to say about finding his wife in bed with someone else. That would surely lose her the moral high ground.'

'Okay, then, so, listen,' Jack continued, patting the air with outstretched palms to prevent further interruption. 'Can you think of anybody you wouldn't mind it being – somebody you could easily forgive? Is there anybody who it would actually be all right for your wife to be carrying on with?'

More shrieks – and not just from Vera – and dark, dirty laughing. Suggestions were thrown into the ring: 'Marlon Brando!' 'Rocky Marciano!' 'Frankie Laine!' Benny suggested James Cagney. Someone said 'Churchill', to which someone else said: 'If we're talking about my missis, it's more likely to be Hitler.' The men all roared. Vera cackled. Then Spanish Joe chipped in with 'Liberace', which brought the house down.

As the laughter settled and faded, Sam asked, 'How about you, Jack?' This created a sudden silence and a change in the temperature.

'Well,' Jack drawled slowly, 'I suppose I could handle finding Renée between the sheets with James Mason. Or Gregory Peck, maybe.'

'No,' said Sam, unsmilingly. 'I mean me finding you with my – absent – missis. With Joyce. It could happen. After all, I'm sure she fancies you.'

The last comment restored the laughter but there was an uncomfortable edge to the moment. Jack shook his head and addressed Sam directly: 'I assume that was meant as a compliment. So thanks, mate,' he said. 'Well, if we're going to limit it to blokes round the table, I'd have to say young Campbell, Joey the Kid, sitting quietly over there. He once told Renée he fancied her. A long time ago when he worked in the shop. D'you remember, Joey?'

'I know what time you're thinking of,' Joey replied. 'But I did not say I fancied her. I said that she was a fine-looking woman. As she was – is. She was putting herself down and I felt she needed flattering.'

'Oh, did you,' said Little Jack Lewis, holding a stare directed at Joey without speaking for a few seconds, and then converting it into a smile. 'As long as *you* weren't putting her down – on that big old sofa we used to have in the upstairs showroom,' Jack said, still smiling. 'And you thought she needed *flattering*? Are you sure that was all? Flattering and not *flattening* her? On her back? On the sofa?'

Vera laughed hysterically at this. The men shifted in their chairs and poured or sipped whisky – except Joey, who kept to orange juice. Vera could not stop laughing – and crying. Fancy Goods Harry put his arm around her shoulders and admonished her fondly. 'Have another Danish,' he said, picking up a pastry from the sideboard. ''Ere, put this in your gob and stop that racket.'

'Oh dear,' Vera said as she took the Danish pastry with one hand and, with the other, wiped away her tears of laughter with a handkerchief.

At this point the thirteen-year-old Ronnie Lewis – who, unnoticed, had been quietly listening to proceedings seated outside the room while sipping a glass of Scotch whisky and lemonade – rose uneasily from his chair and tottered away upstairs.

Seventeen

'Have a good time, everybody. Happy birthday, Sam.' Renée Lewis's farewell remained in Sam Golub's consciousness for days after the whisky-night gathering around that faded oak dining table in the Lewis and Son furniture store's back room. Renée had barely ever shared more than half-a-dozen words with Sam and so it was more than surprising when she presented him with a birthday cake and offered her congratulations.

Was she trying genuinely to cheer him up, he wondered, because of Joyce's departure and lingering absence? And had Little Jack, completely out of character, put her up to it? Or was it all a joke, laughing at him, taking the mickey? Part of a nasty game based on Little Jack's provocative question about coming home and 'finding your missis in bed with another feller'? Calculated to make him feel small and pathetic?

A 'cuckold'. That was Benny's word for it. 'She's making a cuckold of you, Sammy,' Benny had said as the two men sat together in the Astoria café. 'Don't let her. Stay strong. You and Joyce belong together. He's trying to drag her away, that bleedin' little Italian painter. He's not exactly Michelangelo, is he? You know how to deal with him. And if you want help from the Astorians, it's yours. I'm telling you, don't let him make a cuckold of you.'

'*Cuckold*? What does that bloody well mean? What are you on about?' Sam had never heard the word before and was puzzling how to respond to Benny's urging. This was just part of his difficulty in dealing with the whole situation. He didn't need telling that he would be perfectly capable of finding his wife's lover and giving him a good belting, and that Benny the Macher and his Astorians knew very well how to remove the Italian decorator from South London and make sure that he had no chance of returning.

But Sam also realised that he hadn't exactly been easy to live with in recent times. He couldn't control the burning ball of anger that lay inside him, couldn't always stop it from bursting out. And Joyce was first in the line of fire. He needed time to turn over a new leaf and show her that he could do so. But he was still so easily provoked. Anyone could fire him up – as Little Jack had at the whisky-night table.

'Why did I make that stupid remark about him and Joyce?' Sam had repeatedly asked himself, and now, in the Astoria café, was rhetorically asking Benny. 'I just wanted to get back at him, and not by shouting or insulting or threatening. I was really trying, for once, to hold back. Speak quietly. And that was how it came out: "I'm sure she fancies you." Which is bloody ridiculous. Joyce hates Little Jack's guts almost as much as I do.'

'As do most people,' Benny said, standing up from the table. Putting his arm around Sam's shoulders and hugging him. 'Ah, here's the man who'll do the job for you. Lightning fists himself.' Benny released Sam's back and held out his hand in greeting as Joey the Boxer entered the café. 'Here, Joey boy, I've kept the seat warm for you.'

'Wotcher, Sam. Benny, thanks. How are you?'

'Very well, thanks, Joey. I'm just leaving. Gotta relieve Bertha at the shop. She's got to go and meet Simon at the school. Here, sit down. Good luck for the fight next week. Sam and I will be there cheering you on. Poor old Butch, I feel sorry for him. Just two fights to go and you're going to be the champ. I know you are. We all can't wait.'

'Thanks, though I don't know about "all". Ta ta.'

'How's it going, Sam?' Joey inquired as Benny left the café.

'Not too clever, Kiddo. What about you?'

'Oh, I'm in fine fettle, thanks. Got a new girlfriend. Paula.'

'Blimey,' said Sam. 'How do you keep count?'

'No, *really*. I reckon this one's the real thing. I'm thinking about marriage.'

'I wouldn't necessarily recommend it.'

'Oh no, of course. Thoughtless of me. Sorry, Sam.'

'No, no, it's all right. Good luck to you, Kid. Actually, I was just talking to Benny about Little Jack's whisky night when Renée brought in that cake. What was all that about? I've hardly ever spoken to her. And she's hardly ever spoken to me. I can't make her out. And then there was that business about finding your missis in bed with someone. I was wondering if it was all designed to get at me. Taking the piss about Joyce going off with that eyetie painter, leaving me clumping around the house with my stick. It certainly succeeded in getting to me, making me say the first stupid thing that came into my head.'

'Well,' said Joey, 'If you remember, he was also getting at me. Like he always does.'

'Oh, right. Yes. I'd forgotten,' said Sam, suddenly forced to drop his own preoccupation. 'What was all that about you and the mysterious Renée? Did you try to get busy with her?'

'No, well, not exactly. It was her who got busy with me. She was complaining about Little Jack, as she sometimes did – and not just to me. She was upset. He'd apparently told her that, when she had no make-up on, she was an "ugly cow". Her eyes were like "two piss-holes", he said. And I just reassured her, told her Jack was talking a lot of balls and that she was really attractive. And she suddenly starts cryin' on my shoulder, telling me how lovely I am and hugging me tight. And she gives me a big, deep kiss. After that, we used to steal the odd moment in the odd corner of the upstairs showroom for a kiss and cuddle but it never went much further than that. And gradually it petered out and I was on my way, concentrating on my training and keeping fit.

'It wouldn't have been clever going any further,' Joey added. 'Renée is not the most diplomatic of women. She went and told Jack that, "not everyone thinks I'm an ugly cow. Young Joey thinks I'm attractive. *You're a very attractive woman*, he told me."'

'So, there was something in it. Little Jack did have grounds for suspicion. I can't say I blame you, Kid. Renée *is* an attractive woman, although she is a bit flash. She has certainly puzzled me. It's all very well wishing somebody "happy birthday" when you're told about them having a birthday coming up. But she went to a lot of trouble – and I personally never told her it was my birthday. Making me a cake specially and speaking to me in such a friendly way.'

'Maybe,' suggested Joey the Boxer, 'Jack had seen her without her make-up that morning and made one of his typically sweet comments. So maybe she needed someone to feel good towards her. By making them a cake.'

'Yeah, but I don't like cake.'

Eighteen

Since Kid Joey's previous entanglement with Denny 'Butch' Martin, the only time he had been to the Shoreditch Town Hall for a boxing match was as a spectator at his young stablemate Harry Gilbert's astonishing bout against Scotty Brown of Dundee. A somewhat less astonishing memory was that of his girlfriend Sandra walking out on him shortly afterwards.

This time was different – and not just because his latest lady friend had ended their relationship *before* a big occasion at the town hall. This time, Joey would be in the ring himself in a twelve-round title eliminator against Denny Martin, whom he had beaten in their only other contest – a points decision that had Joey a long way ahead. And he was a strong favourite to win this return match, in which both men weighed in at just under 160 pounds. It was the Shoreditch venue's biggest event in a long time.

Benny was, as usual for a Kid Joey fight, in the watching crowd, as was Little Jack. The two men were in prime seats close to but on opposite sides of the ring. Sam sat next to Benny. Maxie the Ganoff, Fancy Goods Harry and Vera were seated two or three rows behind them. A reluctant Simon Pomeranski was at home poring over a pile of homework.

Just before the two fighters entered the arena, a somewhat dishevelled Monty Berman came in and scuttled to a waiting seat just two rows from the ring. 'What a sight,' whispered Sam.

'Well,' Benny answered, 'you know he hardly ever leaves the Fox and he had to manage the last bit of daylight to get here on time – vampires can't deal with that.' And both men laughed, in keeping with the overwhelmingly optimistic mood among Joey's supporters.

Benny had watched Joey's light training session the day before in the Brixton gym. As he'd left, he had passed Little Jack on his way in. Jack briefly acknowledged him by simply stating his name with a casual nod: 'Benny.' And then, after a pause: 'How's he looking?'

'He seems in pretty good nick,' said Benny.

'Oh good,' Jack responded flatly with a frown as he continued into the gym.

Now, just over twenty-four hours later, the two latter-day gladiators were being hailed through the Shoreditch PA system – 'Joseph Reynard Campbell: the Brixton bomber, Kid Joeeeeyah!' and 'Yorkshire's very own butcher boy: the one and only Doncaster Denny "Butch" Maaaartin!' – as they stood either side of the referee in the centre of their heavy-duty canvas battlefield. Denny Martin wore a green silk dressing gown with the words 'Payback Time' emblazoned in large white letters across the back.

The first of the scheduled dozen three-minute rounds started very slowly, a contrast in Joey's case to his normal lightning dash into his opponent's space. The second round was similar, with both fighters cagily exploring the other's defence. In the third, Joey seemed content to defend with his back to the ropes but, as the round came to an end, Butch felt encouraged to attack and caught Joey with a clean uppercut to the chin.

'I can't understand it,' Benny said to Sam. 'What's he doing? Joey can surely murder this feller. He's ten times faster. He's got the man's number. Why is he holding back?' At this point, Benny caught Little Jack's eye. Jack looked perturbed and shook his head from side to side.

And so the contest stuttered on with mostly minimal hostility. Butch caught Joey in the eighth with a straight left to the face when the Kid dropped his guard but little damage was done. And, at the end of the tenth, Joey, the crowd now urging him on, unleashed a barrage of punches to the Yorkshireman's head and body but the bell came to Butch's rescue.

The crowd's impatience grew as Joey failed to resume the onslaught in the eleventh. Vera was on her feet screaming high-pitched exhortations, Benny was making puzzled what's-going-on gestures with his arms, eyes and shoulders, Monty Berman was yawning. And then, the spectators, the majority of them rooting for Joey, were stunned when Butch made contact with another uppercut and Joey sank to the canvas. 'He hardly touched him,' Benny complained. 'Get up,' Vera yelled, and Sam and Maxie both looked as taken aback as Kid Joey apparently was.

In the event, he did get up, well before he could have been counted out. At the bell, his seconds raced to splash and sponge his face. Joey waved them away and stared out into the crowd, who were now making the town hall shake with noise. While Benny and Sam were both animated and urging Joey on, Little Jack was sitting still with his hands in his lap, clasped together. And, once again, he was turning his head from side to side.

And so the bell rang for the final round, at the beginning of which the two boxers touched gloves in the sport's traditional mark of mutual respect and Joey once again took up a defensive stance with his back to the ropes. 'I reckon Martin must be ahead,' said Benny, in the querulous tone of a man expressing the unthinkable. Suddenly, Joey ducked under a looping attempt by Butch to connect to his head and sprinted round the Doncaster man's lumbering frame in an extraordinary burst of speed and energy.

Butch was confused and walked innocently into the first of a spectacular cluster of punches to his head, chin and midriff, and stumbled backwards towards his corner, completely dazed but throwing a token right-hander into the air. As Joey continued the assault, spectators called upon the referee to stop the fight and prevent Butch receiving further pounding. But the referee, Frank Musoe, a local but experienced man, did not intervene.

Eventually and mercifully, Joey put an end to the torture with a right to the chin sending Denny 'Butch' Martin into unconsciousness. As Musoe, against a wall of cheering, began a pointless count over Butch's body and then stopped, Little Jack swiftly got up from his seat and made his way to the exit. 'Look at him,' Fancy Goods said to Vera, 'always has to be the first with the congratulations. I'm surprised he hasn't tried to climb into the ring.'

It took a while for the ringside doctor to bring Butch Martin round and, by the time he was able to stand, Frank Musoe was lifting Joey Campbell's hand and Little Jack Lewis was demanding but being refused entry into Joey's dressing room.

Nineteen

The sound of the doorbell startled Joyce Golub. In the three weeks she had been alone in the flat after her Italian painter boyfriend had left, visitors had been a rarity. The painter, Roberto, had installed the bell – it played, at high volume, the five notes of the song title 'O Sole Mio' – and Joyce loved it so much she would press the bell herself from time to time just to hear it.

But this time was different. She could see a man's shape through the frosted glass of her front-door window and called out nervously: 'Who's that?'

The reply – 'It's me, Jack. Jack Lewis' – increased her nervousness but she felt she couldn't avoid answering. She took a deep breath and undid the latch before opening the door in a manner she hoped would convey at least the appearance of couldn't-careless composure.

'Jack!'

'Hello Joyce.'

'How did you…' She spoke as if each word was a single sentence on its own.

Little Jack held up his hand. 'Oh, I know all about your Italiano painter, decorator and ice-cream man leaving you in the lurchio…'

'Roberto. But he had to…'

'Oh don't try to give him the benefit of the doubt. There is no doubt, Joycey. He's a rat. And a fool.'

'Did Sam give you my address?'

'Poor old Sam, no. You know that I know about most things that happen in South London. It was easy enough to find you. May I come in?'

'Oh, sorry. Yes, of course,' and, as Little Jack stepped through the doorway, which led straight into the living room, 'Would you like a cup of tea?'

'No thanks, darling. I just thought I'd come by and look in to see how you're getting on now you're on your own. And I brought a little present,' he said, as he reached into the bag he was carrying – and produced a half-bottle of champagne.

'Here, try this. Makes a very nice change from tea. I'd love to have a glass with you and I knew you'd offer me a cuppa, being the hospitable person you are, so I didn't bring a whole bottle. That would've looked a bit presumptuous.'

'That's very thoughtful of you, Jack. How did you know I wasn't working today?'

'I didn't. Just took a chance. It's not exactly far to drive and it's quick at this time of day. I parked just round the corner. I came because I was… concerned about you. That you might feel lonely. Now that the eyetie's done a runner.'

'Roberto. His name's Roberto.'

'*Rob*erto,' Jack mispronounced the name, putting the emphasis on the first syllable, '*Rob*erto's done a runner.'

'Jack, he hasn't done a runner. We were over. Finished. The relationship had run its course. And Roberto had commitments in Italy.'

'Well, most people's opinion is that he had a big commitment in England – to you. What kind of bloke runs off from a beautiful woman like you?'

'Oh, please, Jack. Do me a favour…'

'No, I mean it. You are a very good-looking woman.'

'No I'm not. But thank you, anyway. He's got kids,' Joyce said, before lighting a cigarette and holding out her cigarette case towards Little Jack.

'No thanks, darlin'. I stick to cigars these days. But if you've got a couple of glasses I'll open the champagne.' And, as Joyce exhaled, stood up from the table at which she and Little Jack sat opposite each other, and brought out a pair of drinking glasses from a cupboard and placed them on the table, Little Jack continued: 'Kids, eh. Roberto the rascal! Well, at least you've seen the back of him. Good riddance. He won't be coming back to London again.'

'How can you be sure?'

'I told you. I know these things. And I can help you, Joycey. I'm a lucky man and I'm in a position to help you now you're on your own. Just say the word. Cheers!'

'Cheers.' Joyce smiled weakly and grasped her glass without lifting it as Jack held his up high.

'Come on, girl. Drink up.' And, as she hesitantly lifted her glass, he leaned across the table and clinked his glass against hers: 'Chin, chin. And I mean it, if there's anything you need, promise you'll tell me.'

'That's very kind of you, Jack, but I'm speaking to someone at the end of the week about a job. It's not that far and is quite well paid.'

'Well, as I say, the offer's there. D'you mind if I take my drink over to the sofa? This expensive-looking chair of yours is very uncomfortable for my back – I was going to say "no hard feelings" but as it happens that is just what I've got, hard feelings in my back.'

Joyce smiled at this as she replied. 'Of course. It's probably better sitting there anyway with the coffee table in front of you. And you can put your glass on one of the doyleys.'

'*Our* glasses, please. Surely you're not going to stay sitting up there while I'm down here? There are two doyleys after all. And an ashtray.'

'Of course,' she said, and took a sip of champagne before sitting down and placing her glass carefully on to the vacant small, round lace mat and just as carefully putting her cigarette into the ashtray.

'Cheers, here's to you!' Jack again clinked glasses. Joyce humoured him with another, wordless smile.

'I'm very fond of you, Joyce,' said Jack, as Joyce took a second sip from her glass. 'Don't know if you realise how much.'

'Well it's always good to be friends.' Joyce said, putting down her glass.

'He edged a little closer to her as he next spoke. 'Yes it is. And to be more than friends is very, very good.'

'Yes, I suppose so. But what do you mean?'

'Sam himself told me you felt something for me. Something romantic.'

'*What?*'

'Yes, he told me. I suppose I was unable to hide that I fancy you and so he revealed that you fancy me.'

Little Jack stroked Joyce's face and pulled her into an embrace.

'Jack. No! Please.'

'That's the word I want to hear. The one word above all: "*Please*".'

Twenty

Jeffrey Johnson Calloway was pleased that, as he was leaving England and on his way to the West Indies, thousands of others in recent years had travelled – and were still travelling – in the opposite direction. He had always chosen to celebrate his individuality rather than follow the crowd and he had enjoyed considerable success in doing so. But now, looking forward to a new life in the sunshine, and perhaps a new line of business – he had arranged to meet a man about a possible opening in the cloth trade, which sounded promising – each new mile further away from Southampton made him relax a little more.

The SS *North Star*, of the Elders and Fyffes line, was a banana boat. It had unloaded its stock of bananas at Southampton a fortnight earlier and was returning now to Kingston, Jamaica, with a cargo of washing machines – and paying passengers. The latter were distributed through the *North Star*'s twelve first-class cabins, in one of which Jeff Calloway liked to lie on his bed listening to crew members outside on the deck warbling their own adaptations of Caribbean songs – *It was under de coconut tree / Dat she made love wid me,* or a variant of 'Come Back, Liza': *When me think o' Jamaica / Water come a me eye.*

During the early hours of the journey, he frequently found himself troubled by thoughts of England, but as the *North Star* nosed its way to the home of his forefathers, he determined to earn himself a new living. After all, there were no agreeable prospects for him in the UK and the love affair upon which he had placed such high hopes had ended disastrously and it was his own stupid fault.

He had met a woman at a house party in Clapham and warmed to her immediately. She had described herself as a 'businesswoman' but, throughout a six-month relationship, Jeff never found out precisely what kind of business she was in. 'Oh, you know, this and that, export and import, the way of the modern world,' she'd say and when he probed, she easily diverted him, remarking that her day-to-day labours, along with the many meetings she had to attend, were 'far too boring to interest you'. And she told him that he had given her hope of a new and exciting life in which she could leave her boring job behind.

Then, after they had been to a restaurant in Soho where their waitress spent what Jeff's girlfriend described as an 'intrusive' amount of time chatting to them as they were eating, he went back the following week on his own, making sure he sat at the same table, served by the same waitress. A few days later, an attachment secured, walking with the waitress in a Soho street – a bit too brazen maybe, no more than a hundred yards from the businesswoman's mystery office – there was a scene. Businesswoman recognised waitress; recognised, too, his way of charming her, shuffling walk, boyish grin. And now, a month later, he was on his way to Jamaica.

As the *North Star* approached Kingston Harbour, Jeff smiled at the recollection. 'She was so sweet, my little waitress. She ruined my chance of a good marriage but she wasn't to know. I was a fool but it was already going wrong. It was not to be. Now I am definitely doing the right thing,' he said out loud as he lifted his suitcases from the side of his bed and took one last look around the cabin, checking the drawers and the space under the bed.

Shortly afterwards, as he stepped out on to the deck, a pair of customs officers approached. One of them held out his hand and Jeff shook it as the man greeted him in clipped, staccato English: 'You Mister Jeffrey Calloway?'

In all the strange newness of his situation, Jeff was suddenly confused. He looked around towards the harbour and up into the translucent sky above the pulsating mass of humanity below, his mind a blank page awaiting inscription. His head spun with the panorama of colours, the roar and richness of sounds and aromas. The customs officer's voice jolted him back: 'Mister Calloway?'

'Yes? Oh I am sorry, yes I am Calloway, Jeff, Jeffrey Calloway.'

The customs man smiled and continued: 'You Mister Solomons guest. He speak for you already. We no need trouble you. Welcome to Kingston, Jamaica.' And he smiled even wider as his colleague saluted Jeff. Neither of the officers so much as glanced at Jeff's passport.

He had been told to look out for Lionel Solomons on the quayside when the *North Star* docked. It shouldn't be difficult, they said. Solomons was an exuberant man who dressed and behaved in extravagant fashion. As the boat came near to land, people of all shapes, sizes, ages and complexions could be seen, some of them standing by idly while others ran this way and that, calling out and acknowledging orders issued in relation to the *North Star*'s progress through the harbour.

But once Jeff, standing near the prow, gazing at the crowd milling around the water's edge, fixed his eyes on Lionel Solomons, white-suited over a pair of two-tone brown-and-cream brogues and theatrically waving a large white panama hat, everybody else seemed to merge into a kind of black-and-white cinematic background behind the technicolor man he was to meet.

As soon as the passengers disembarked, Solomons strode forward, waving his hat and repeating the phrase he had used to sweeten the customs officers: 'That boy's my guest. Treat him nicely. That boy there,' he added for the benefit of the porters and cabin staff, 'in that very serious, dark Great British suit.' Though around six inches shorter than Jeffrey Calloway, Lionel Solomons seemed to swamp the newcomer as he pumped his hand and put his arm around him in proprietorial fashion, having restored the panama to the crown of his head.

'Jeffrey,' he cried, removing his arms from his guest in order to look him in the face and sweep the air with an expansive gesture. 'You're looking marvellous.' And he winked. 'Did you have a good trip? It's good to see you. Welcome to Kingston, Jamaica.' All in a loud, laughing Caribbean cadence with a faint, but noticeable, East European accent.

'It's so nice of you to put me up in your house until I get settled,' said Jeff. 'You seem to have quite a reputation, especially for being kind and generous.'

'Ah, that's really because me wife Irene is a hospitable lady,' Lionel said, and laughed rhythmically. 'Oh, everybody knows old Uncle Lionel,' he continued, his arm around Jeff Alexander's shoulder again. *Everybody*. All over Kingston.'

Twenty-one

It was said that Sam 'the Stick' Golub never recovered from the shock of returning from the jaunt in Bournemouth to an empty home and that, for months afterwards, he always carried with him, in a little cloth bag, a pair of diamond earrings he had saved for his wife from the Farringdon haul. He managed to get a couple of messages to her, saying he had 'learned a lesson' and would give up all 'unlawful business' if she came back. But Joyce remained resolute, even when her Italian boyfriend left her after eight weeks of their setting up home together in Beckenham, on the Kentish side of South London.

'Ah, poor, mixed-up Sammy,' Joyce Golub said with a sigh, putting down her cup of tea. 'I wanted to give him a child. A son. Poor bastard. He really wanted a boy,' she told her best friend. 'You know, Bertha, I am struggling to admit to myself that it wasn't the freedom that brought me such a strong feeling of relief. It certainly couldn't be freedom that has brought me such sadness. And guilt.

'If I am honest with myself – really, really honest – it's something more definite. Specific. And it'll sound cruel to you, I know. The fact is…' And Joyce Golub broke off to allow a breath to emerge from somewhere deep inside her. 'It's such a *relief*,' she said, picking up the thread, 'not to have to live my life protecting that man, a cripple, from himself, and from the shame he feels at having to rely on a stick, a piece of wood, to get around. To function.'

The corner table at which Joyce Golub and Bertha Pomeranski were seated in the Astoria café might well have been the same one at which Benny and Estelle had sat two years earlier. It was the first time Joyce had been back in Brixton since she and her painter, Roberto, had moved into the flat in which he had been living alone – and which he had left without either warning her or paying that month's rent.

'We used to have such fun during the war, remember? You, Benny, me and Sam,' said Joyce, allowing herself a smile. 'The way he used to dance – like he was trying to shake off his great big cloud of resentment. But I loved it. The scrapes I got him out of! As did you and Benny, of course. But lately he's got more and more bitter. Before I left, he was bad and I think he's still bad, or even worse. I think he's still got a couple of guns – you remember he had that collection of guns, about half-a-dozen of 'em?'

'Of course, he gave Benny a couple.'

'That's right. He promised me he was getting rid of them but I think he's still got – or *had* when I was still living with him – a couple. And now I'm worried he's going to injure or even kill somebody one of these days. Or get seriously hurt... though... that may be what he deserves. Or needs.'

Bertha leaned forward and squeezed her friend's hand. 'Oh, Joycey,' she said, plaintive and compassionate. 'It's so sad to hear you saying that. Sam's in a terrible way – has been since you left. He just drifts aimlessly these days. You've got to feel sorry for him.'

'I do, Berth, I do. Honest. But that's all it is: pity. All it ever has been. God knows, I've shown great concern for him. Given him so much attention. A few years ago, he had some dreadful pain in his leg. The stick wasn't enough and I had to help him walk everywhere. I've cosied up to him when we watched the telly. Cuddled him. Shown him a lot of physical affection...'

She took another deep breath before continuing: 'I sometimes wonder if all the hugging and holding hands is a way of avoiding proper, loving care because that's so much harder. It's difficult. It's demanding. Instead of giving him a squeeze, which requires very little effort, maybe I should have found out more about how I could help him, speak to doctors, get advice, get pills or something, check what kind of chair he needs to sit on, what kind of bed to sleep in, sort out holidays, learn to drive, help more in the business.'

'Luckily,' said Bertha after taking a sip of tea, 'Sam's businesses more or less run themselves. His two shops in Brixton both have excellent managers. Which is just as well, for you. Well,' Bertha stumbled, realising that she seemed to be chastising Joyce, 'for him, of course. For both of you. But, listen, how are *you* managing? Especially now Roberto's gone back to Italy. That must be really upsetting.'

'A little. But it was never going to work long-term. We had fun. He made me feel like a woman again. For a change, I was the one being helped all the time instead of being the helper. I'll always be grateful to him for giving me a way out of my life with Sam. And it wasn't his actual leaving that hurt. He's Italian and wanted to return to Italy – where, I found out from his young assistant decorator, he has a wife and two kids…'

'What?'

'Yes, but it wasn't that that got to me. It was what I thought of as the cheapness of leaving me with the rent unpaid. But then, I found out, while he had been paying the rent, he'd also been sending money home to her.

'And I'm managing pretty well, I think. That's what I was meaning to tell you. I've got a job. At a furniture firm in Bromley. Helping in the office and a little bit in the shop, too. It's like Bromley's version of Little Jack's, you could say. But classier stuff. A lot of it comes from Italy, funnily enough. And my boss – he's called Mike Harman – is a much nicer feller than Jack Lewis. And he's Jewish!'

'Really? And single, I suppose.'

'Oh no, it's nothing like that. He's happily married with kids. I've met his wife, Helen. Turns out she's distantly related to Spanish Joe.'

'No! Oh well, it sounds like you've fallen on your feet. So glad you're doing well. Wish I could say the same for your old man. He wanders around with a face like a wet night in Warsaw.' Bertha paused and looked at Joyce with a seriously-concerned-friend face. 'He misses you terribly,' Bertha said. And then it was her turn to sigh.

'Well, as I've said, I do feel sorry for him.' Joyce countered Bertha's seriously-concerned face with the determined expression of a woman who is 'doing quite well, thank you, despite the circumstances'. She didn't say that, but pressed her lips together as if to stop any weakness or sympathy for her husband leaking out. 'I still recall the good times and miss them,' she said, after a minute or two, 'but they are long gone. For a long time, Sam with his perishing stick has been much more angry than he has been happy. And a lot of that anger is towards himself.'

'Men, eh?' Bertha's comment was intended to ward off another awkward pause, or a further slide into despair.

But it prompted Joyce to continue: 'He thinks of himself as bigshot material but he is never going to outsmart Little Jack Lewis – not to mention your Benny. As for Jack… Sorry. Berth, I suddenly need the lav. Could you order me a Bakewell to go with my tea?'

Joyce returned, slightly red-eyed, just as the waitress was putting her Bakewell tart on the table. 'Oh, thanks, Berth. That's grand. Let's settle up at the end.'

'You were saying,' said Bertha. 'Something about Little Jack.'

'Oh, no, nothing, except he got in touch offering to help me. I said I didn't need it. I… I was just saying that Sam's ambition seemed to be to become a Mister Big like Little Jack. Not a nice ambition. But Sam seemed to almost admire violence. And the strange thing is, I believe he has a truly warm heart deep down. All this fighting talk and determination not to let anyone put one over on him – it's all to do with his accident, his leg, I'm sure. I never used to feel threatened physically by Sam. We practically grew up together. But in recent times, I have felt frightened. A couple of times, I have felt that he was about to hit me. But, up to now at least, he still hasn't.'

'Oh, he never would, I'm sure,' said Bertha, her smile reassuring. 'In fact, I agree that he did seem to get more and more bitter, especially after you, well, went away. But since you've gone, he's slowed down a great deal. I would even say he's gone a bit soft…'

Joyce's raised eyebrows signalled the unlikeliness of such a radical transformation, but Bertha pressed on regardless: 'No, really. Even Benny's commented on it. He's slowed down. He misses you so much. He told Benny that he needs you.'

Bertha sat back in her chair before continuing. 'It's not exactly a bed of roses for me, with Benny,' she said. 'And that bloody Estelle Davis. He doesn't even pretend any more. At our anniversary party, I couldn't help thinking he was celebrating with her and not with me. She practically took over as the hostess. He can also get angry, believe me. Like a cornered animal. It's not only Sam. It's men, I'm telling you. *Men*.

'And yet, deep down,' Bertha continued, 'Benny is a good man – and a clever one. Things might have been different if his parents hadn't taken him out of school, but they needed the money. Those East End boys, you know, Benny, Sam, Maxie … they were affected deeply by the poverty of their childhoods. *Our* childhoods, too, but men take it differently. They're less accepting, less practical. They were angry about the unfairness.'

'Yes, I know, Berth. Sam has a lot of anger in his heart, but there is also room for love. When we got married, he so wanted a child. A boy. So he could show his son how tough he was, how his injured leg would never be allowed to hold him back.'

'And now he's just fading away without you.'

'I'm sorry, Bertha, I am not going back.'

But she did go back. A few months later, when Sam was unable to drag himself out of bed for three days after one of those 'excellent' shop managers in Brixton made off with a pile of cash and a certain amount of the stock.

Around the same time, Joyce's employer Mike Harman had similar problems with his Italian sources and declared himself bankrupt. And Joyce lost her job.

Twenty-two

Lionel Solomons lived in Sandhurst Crescent, a smart part of Kingston, with his wife Irene. 'Irene and me,' Lionel would say, 'we're like the peas in the whistles,' by which he meant the house was too big for the two of them now that the children had grown up and gone away. Their daughter, Yvonne, had gone to music school, got married and was living in America. Their son, Rudy, was in England. 'The peas in the whistles' was one of those quirky phrases of Lionel's that, right from the start of their relationship, was guaranteed to make Jeff Calloway laugh.

When Jeff arrived at the house, it impressed him enormously, especially as he was being invited to make it his home for as long as was necessary. The two living rooms were both very large and there were four bedrooms. At the front was an imposing wooden fretwork verandah with a hammock suspended from its roof. On his first evening in Kingston, Jeff sat outside on the verandah with Lionel, drinking Red Stripe beer that Irene brought out to them and which Lionel opened by cracking the caps off the bottles against a nail on the wall.

Lionel and Irene ran a clothing store on Orange Street, near the Coronation Market. It was successful enough but shopkeeping was a little too quiet a life for Lionel. He carried on various strands of 'extra' business, the details of which he kept hidden from Irene. She was reasonably content with this arrangement and asked no embarrassing questions since it kept them comfortable and enabled her to keep up a certain style among the ladies of her coffee-and-cards set.

It also enhanced Lionel's status in virtually every stratum of Jamaican life. Never a man for keeping his head down, he made full use of his talent for ingratiating himself with the authorities. He needed to: in 1950s and 1960s Kingston, nearly every aspect of Lionel's 'extra' business, from fixing races at Knutsford Park to running errands for some very unsavoury American gang bosses, required someone, somewhere, to turn a blind eye.

But he was a genuinely warm and kind man as well as a 'flexible' one when it came to interpreting the law, and he was probably the most popular person on the island. He had arrived there from Warsaw in the 1930s intending to go on to the United States but, having made himself known to the island's then Jewish spiritual leader, Rabbi Silverman, who was also a relative newcomer to Jamaica, Lionel was introduced to a handful of Kingston's Jewish families and he liked what he saw. They were open, worldly, generous, ready to reach out and take an interest in others. It was all such a contrast to his own family back home, where everyone seemed to huddle in corners in fear and where his grandfather was treated like a king because he was a Talmud scholar, even though he was a miserable old wretch who seldom smiled or spoke to his grandchildren except to reprimand them.

It wasn't long before Lionel met Irene Gubbay, the daughter of a wealthy local fruit merchant, and the idea of America was abandoned for good. Their wedding was a grand affair, which stopped the traffic for miles around the town hall. Lionel was launched as a citizen of note and he never looked back.

Jeff Calloway's introduction into this environment was somewhat different. Whereas the young Lionel had sat up into the night exchanging stories about himself and his Polish home and family with the local Jews who proudly told him about various Jewish men and women in the town – and in its cemetery – Jeff, a far more private person, was pleased that nobody, apart from Lionel and Irene, seemed particularly interested in him.

He started work as an assistant in Lionel's store, Solomons Clothing, and later helped Lionel with the 'extra' stuff. He learned quickly and seemed to thrive on the clandestine nature of it all. With money in his pocket, he began to stride around town and, in cavalier fashion, quickly ran through a succession of three or four girlfriends. He also developed a taste for the local liquor and liked to order a 'Q' of white or red rum for himself and the friends he quickly made.

Solomons Clothing was a barn of a place. Jeff loved the smell and the feel of the material, laid out in rolls on the counter and in smaller strips hanging up at the back of the shop. He loved the style of the place, the easy-going, lively way Lionel would entertain his 'regulars' – sad, elderly or just plain dubious types, many of them, who came in off Orange Street simply to pass the time of day, never to buy anything, not even a card of buttons or a pair of shoelaces.

There was a tailor on hand – it was old George Peller for years, a small, bent, sallow-faced man, tape-measure perpetually round his neck like a prayer shawl – and always one of a series of small boys employed as a 'runner' or 'fetcher'. Lionel was always kind to them and gave them sweets, though he paid them little. Some were playing hooky from school.

One of these boys – a little, nut-brown, smiling sparrow of a lad called Clyde – was twice hauled out by a man from the school board. But he always came back to Solomons Clothing. He started off working an hour a day after school; then he worked before school and eventually during school hours. One day, however, there was an accident.

Running like a crazy, wild bird, as he always did, along the nearby wharf, Clyde slipped, hit his head and was engulfed by the harbour waters. Jeff was shocked to find himself as emotionally overcome by this terrible misfortune as if the boy had been a close member of his own family. Perhaps paradoxically, the experience helped him to find the inner strength necessary to finally shake off his old existence and embrace the new – his new home and new Jamaican life.

Within weeks of arriving in Jamaica, Jeff Calloway was living in one of the best parts of town, making new friends, male and female, still shuffling, still grinning in that old way of his. He became a devotee of cricket and calypso. He worked hard in Lionel and Irene's employment and liked to say that the job fitted him like a good suit, the kind that they made up and sold in the store, the kind that Lionel himself wore, snappy but comfortable. And, despite his fondness for rum and beer, Jeff kept himself fit by regularly running, swimming and, two years into his Jamaican life, joining the local cricket and tennis club.

Lionel was pleased and amused by Jeff's rapid acclimatisation and did not interfere with him except occasionally to counsel a little restraint. 'I understand how you feel,' he said, 'and I'm pleased with what you're doing for me, especially in the shop. Outside the shop, you are going a little too fast, especially,' he said with a laugh, 'with the ladies. Take it easy. You are welcome to lodge with Irene and me permanently, as long as you like. But if and when you find a new apartment, I'll increase your wages so you'll be able to pay the rent. But first you need to slow down.' At which point, Lionel's smile erupted into laughter.

But, by now, Jeff was too full of enthusiasm for his new life to slow down. He worked hard, travelled to almost every part of the island and was determined to enjoy every hour of every day, especially the leisure hours. There was a period when he spent almost every evening in the Sombrero club, near the harbour. It was one of his favourite places in the whole of Jamaica and he enjoyed many good times there with his friends. He was on good terms with the owner and the staff always made a fuss of him. He spent freely and virtually had the run of the place, the best table, the most lavish food, the finest booze and, if he ever needed an escort, the best-looking women. But two separate nights there – a month or so apart – changed things.

The first was one Friday night when a young fellow was in the club trying to impress the girl he had brought along. It had taken his whole week's wages but, as he proudly told his friends, he was 'really hot' for this 'princess' and he was determined to show her the best time. He'd bought himself a white suit and was feeling sharp – if virtually broke. In the Sombrero, he unwittingly sat himself and his date down at the table that Jeff always liked to occupy.

The club was busy and the waitress who served them was new and didn't know about Jeff Calloway's special privileges. The manager was away and, by the time Jeff arrived with a couple of business acquaintances, somehow nobody had noticed that these two young people were halfway through their meal, joking and sweet-talking at a larger-than-regular table.

It certainly was not part of the eager young *bwoy*'s plans to have his dignity stripped from him in front of his new girlfriend, particularly when things seemed to be going so well. And so he put up a spirited show when Jeff asked him to leave the table – at first politely – 'I'm terribly sorry, folks, but this table is reserved for me.'

'But the waitress said it was available.'

'I'm afraid the waitress was wrong. She's new and didn't consult the reservations list.'

'We've been here for some time. We got food on our plates, drink in our glasses. I'm not movin''

And then, still polite, Jeff called over the deputy manager – but the young man was immovable: 'Go away and let us finish. You are givin' me indigestion.' Which prompted the deputy manager to suggest a compromise: 'Shall we say twenty minutes? If you'd like to wait in the bar in the meantime, Mr Calloway, the drinks will be on the house.'

'No,' insisted the white-suited Romeo at the table, 'we don't want minutes. We want hours.'

Turning to his two business associates, Jeff said, in that same polite fashion, 'I do apologise, gentlemen. Would you please excuse me for a moment?' And, turning to the young would-be lover boy with a sigh and a shake of his head, Jeff lifted him out of his chair from behind and marched him out of the club into the car park, his terrified young date scampering along behind. The boy tried to resist but only succeeded in falling to the ground and scuffing the knees of his new suit. Jeff left them both at the entrance and, still in the same restrained tone, ignoring the shouting of the boy and the screaming of the girl, suggested they 'go home. I'll settle your bill.'

Back inside the Sombrero, with the senior staff fussing like mother hens around Jeff and his entourage, things quickly got back to normal. In the rumpus, however, Jeff had accidentally knocked over a rum cocktail at a nearby table and it had spilled on to the pale, lemon-coloured dress of a shy, soulful-eyed young woman, Marie Valentine, out for the night with her friend Julie.

'I'm so sorry, Miss,' said Jeff. 'Send me the bill for the cleaning and, for now, please let me buy you a drink.'

'No, no, it's quite all right. It's nothing, honestly.'

The way she spoke, in a more careful, well-brought-up way than that of the girls he normally encountered in the Sombrero, intrigued and attracted Jeff. 'Please,' he said, 'I insist.'

Marie was still shaking her head when Julie nudged her. 'Come on,' Julie whispered, 'man's only trying to do the right thing.'

So the two girls joined Jeff's table and Jeff, having dutifully introduced Marie and Julie to his associates, gradually drew them out, directing most of his attention towards Marie. This was the first time she had been in the Sombrero. It had been Julie's idea. It would be a laugh, she'd said. 'And now my dress is ruined,' said Marie, a little playfully, her reserve slowly breaking down.

'Oh, I'm sure the cleaners will fix it,' Jeff assured her. 'And if they can't, you get yourself along to Solomons's store in Orange Street and buy a replacement dress on my account. Where'd you get the dress, anyway?'

'Nathan's on King Street. I work there.'

'I knew I'd seen you before. It must have been in Nathan's.'

At this point, their conversation was interrupted by the noisy return of the thwarted young fellow in the white suit, which was more than a little muddy by now. One way and another, Jeff Calloway was clearly not respecting people's clothing that night.

The bruised young lover was yelling: 'You can't just come in here and do a thing like that to me. I'm telling you, man, you'll be sorry.' It had been an hour since Jeff had dumped the young dude on his white-suited backside and he wondered where the cheeky *bwoy* had been and how he had managed to get back into the club. Standards were slipping, it seemed.

Where the angry *bwoy* had been was at his date's mother's place, to try to get the girl calmed down and claim back some of the courting credit he had built up by taking her for a meal at a good table at the Sombrero. How he had got back into the place was anybody's guess but here he was, shouting and pointing his finger.

'Get this bum out of here,' Jeff instructed a heavy from the security team standing by an adjoining table, a bulky, menacing individual who was clearly uncomfortable in the smart but too-tight outfit into which he had been forced. He now looked considerably relieved to have something to do with his hands.

As the security heavy and one of the club's bouncers together removed the excitable young man – this time for good – he continued to wag his finger and scream at Jeff: 'I'll get you for this, man. You just wait!'

Returning to his seat, Jeff nodded and smiled in an unperturbed way and apologised again to Marie. 'I am so sorry your first experience of this fine establishment has been so disrupted,' he said. 'You must let me bring you back here tomorrow evening for dinner. Saturday is always the best night at the Sombrero. The manager will be back and there's no chance of him letting in any riff-raff.'

Marie had been planning to see her mother the following evening. She wouldn't mind a postponement of that until after church on Sunday. Julie had a date, so Marie would be free. So why not, she thought. It would be a busy Saturday in Nathan's and she'd be on her feet all day. She would appreciate a bit of wining and dining afterwards.

Sure enough, that Saturday evening in the club was pleasantly unruffled, and subsequent evenings, and afternoons, not only at the Sombrero, but also the White Parrot and other spots around the island were just as enjoyable. Jeff found himself enchanted by Marie. She was so much more demure than the other local young women he knew; she was intelligent, and she clearly seemed interested in him. Perhaps, Jeff thought, he would be able to slow down and settle at last – and reduce the time and money he spent at the clubs and restaurants. He was as happy as he had ever been.

But, a month or so later, when Jeff and Marie had just left the Sombrero at around midnight on a Thursday, as they crossed the street, a man stepped out of a car parked alongside a clump of palms. His sudden movement startled Marie and, turning, she saw that the man was holding a pistol. She screamed, which in turn caused Jeff to grab her arm and start to run. As they both set off, the man fired a single shot. Jeff felt the impact of the blast, which clipped his arm just above the elbow and temporarily deafened him in one ear, but was able to keep running. Marie was still screaming and people in the neighbourhood were yelling. Lights came on in various windows. Cars accelerated. Drivers pressed hard on their horns. The gunman appeared to take fright and scrambled back into his own vehicle and drove away at speed.

Jeff rested and thought things over for a few days. He could not be sure whether or not the gunman was the white-suited dude from the Sombrero – his face had been obscured by the darkness and the palms. The trouble was that, since arriving and establishing himself in Jamaica, Jeff Calloway had put himself about vigorously and, above and beyond the angry young *bwoy* hoping to get his own back, there were already quite a few others who might have wanted to settle a score.

Twenty-three

When Joyce came back to Sam, having helped him through his illness and then agreed to stay, it gave him a new spring in his, albeit disfigured step. But their first conversation, once she had hung up her coat on its old, familiar hook, had not been easy.

'I've had a lot of time to think,' he told her, 'and I know it's been hard going for you being married to me. I've never really appreciated how much you've supported me.

'You see, ever since that thing happened to my leg, I've always tried to ignore it. Be like everyone else, not a cripple who can't do things. Better, in fact. I've always wanted to be better than everyone else, and since I've been on my own in bed, without you, feeling weak, I've thought about it and come to realise I've been stupid. And I'm so happy you're back here with me. I've thought a lot about the good times we had in the war, also with Berth and Benny—'

'So've I,' Joyce chipped in.

'Come 'ere,' Sam said, standing and leaving his stick on a chair. 'Give us a hug.' And she did.

'Nobody is ever gonna change me,' Sam continued, 'not even you, my darlin', but I'm never gonna stop loving you.'

'Oh, Sammy.'

And they held each other again, feeling each other's tears on their faces.

'I've had enough of all that petty crime, pinchin' and pushin'. But I will do what needs to be done, what's right, whatever it takes. Benny's been round quite a bit. He brought Bertha with him a couple of times. Have you had visitors since... well, since you've been on your own, like...' And Sam sighed with all the breath he could muster.

Joyce tried to be cheerful. 'I've seen quite a bit of Bertha,' she said. 'A few others. Oh, and flipping Little Jack even came round to see if he could help.'

'Oh no.'

'No, it was all right.'

'It couldn't have been. Nothing's all right with that bastard. Mister bloody big with his airs and graces. Condescending to the ordinary beings he lords it over, giving orders. Telling them what to do. Holding court and *advising* his gang of hangers-on, helping people with problems. *He's* the problem. He whipped some young kid round the face with a pistol last week. Stupid kid who works for him. Practically blinded the poor idiot. He needs cutting down to size.'

Sam had turned away from Joyce and stared at the carpet as he was making this speech but now he lifted his head and turned back to her: 'How many times did he come to see you?'

'Just the once,' Joyce said, faltering. 'To see if I was okay... then he came back again and rang the doorbell but I pretended not to be in and didn't answer the door... he left a pack of smoked salmon, of all things, in a bag, on the step...'

She sat down, breathing heavily.

'What did he want, that piece of shit?' Sam was finding it hard to keep control of himself.

'I told you. He said he wanted to see how I was getting on. Said he'd heard I was on my own.'

Joyce swallowed as Sam's voice grew louder. 'Of course he knew you were on your own. He got rid of your fancy boyfriend.'

'Got rid of?' Joyce would have screamed if she had the strength.

'Yes. Escorted him off the manor and warned him never to come back. The kind of warning you take very seriously. Doing me a favour apparently, he told Benny. Maybe if he hadn't done that, you'd still be together in your cosy little love nest with Mario Lanza.'

'I thought you meant…'

'What? That Little bloody Jack had done him in? Still caring, still wanting to be with him are you, your little mambo Italiano?'

'No, Sam, no. It was over well before he left. It was never going to last. It was to spite you, to try to forget you and get over you and have a break from how awful you'd been to me before your bloody boys' holiday in Bournemouth… teach you a lesson.'

'So Jack Lewis wanted to help you out, did he? I bet he bloody did. Did he try it on? Did he touch you?'

Joyce sank back down in her chair and cried.

'Did he? Did he lay hands on you?'

Joyce didn't say anything but shook her head and then, eventually, uttered a quiet, feeble, 'no'.

Sam turned his back, hung his head and picked up his stick for support. Joyce stood up, put her arms around him from behind and spoke into his ear: 'I do love you, Sammy. You're the only man I've ever really loved. And now, a bit to my surprise, I still do.'

'I'm sorry.' Sam's voice was husky. 'For everything. It's just that man, that arsehole. People say I'm bad but they don't know me. They don't know what bad is. Real bad. I've been around Benny Pomeranski enough these many years to know not to harm anyone unless they deserve it. I'm not bad. That man is truly bad, Little Jack Arsehole. He's worse than bad. He's evil. He has even somehow managed to spoil this moment of my great happiness, having you back. I can't bear the thought of him putting his slimy hands on you.'

'There's no need to worry on that score. Let's say no more about it. I want you, no one else, especially not a vile piece of work like Little Jack Lewis.' And she looked into his face. And he was softened.

Twenty-four

When Lionel Solomons died, in January 1972, a lot of places fell silent. His funeral was not as grand as his wedding had been, though it was hardly quiet. The group of American men in dark glasses and gleaming mohair suits caught the eye as they gathered under a blazing sun outside the Shaare Shalom Synagogue, serving the United Congregation of Israelites, in Duke Street, Kingston.

Passers-by stopped to watch as the cortège snaked its way to the burial ground in Orange Street, preceded by an odd assortment of musicians including a cornet-player from New Orleans and a klezmer fiddler. Together, they produced a seductive wailing sound, in which the occasionally recognisable melody – including 'Eli, Eli' and Israel's national anthem 'Hatikvah' (Lionel had been a big giver to the Jewish state) – was quickly drowned as if by a chorus of shrieking ghosts.

At the cemetery, Irene was supported on one side by her son Rudy Solomons and on the other by Jeffrey Calloway. After the burial, Rudy, Irene and her daughter Yvonne sat on adjacent chairs holding hands as the line of men passed in front of them, kissing their cheeks or squeezing their shoulders, offering condolences, most of the Americans without removing their dark glasses.

Later, at the house in Sandhurst Crescent, Rudy and Jeff sank bottle after bottle of Red Stripe beer together. Some of the visitors had still not come out from behind their dark glasses, even inside

Irene's kitchen, where Rudy and Jeff sat drinking at the table. One of the men, a New Yorker whose face Jeff recognised but whose name he could not remember, came over to them. The man clearly knew who they were.

'Jeff,' he cried out in greeting, locking Lionel Solomons's erstwhile protégé in a hug. 'Rudy!' The son was given a firm pat on the cheek. 'How are things in England?'

'They're fine,' answered Solomons the younger.

'Yeah,' said the American. 'London's a great city. I'm sure the two of you guys have a lot to talk about in that respect. Rudy, your father was a good man. And a successful one. Nice family, nice cars, clothes, nice place here to live in. He'll leave a big, gaping hole in the island. Don't you want to come over here and fill it?'

'No, not me. I'm settled in London.'

'Ah, that's a shame. Still, I'm sure you know what you're doing. You strike me as a bright guy. Your old man always said that about you. And I hear you've done a heap of studying. Maybe you'll be a professor. I also hear that you and your mother are planning to sell the store.'

'That's right but the name will remain.'

'That's good. That's good. And how about you, Jeff? I can remember you working in that store. You got me that bombazine, remember? I had a wild dress made for my old lady outta the stuff. The old days, eh? Well, you're your own man, now. Doing pretty well, I hear. You don't want to get too big, though, do you? Life can get hard and I know you like the good life out here. You see, Rudy,' he said, half-turning to the younger man, 'not everybody is in such a hurry to get back to good old England.'

The suits didn't stay around long and once the other visitors had filed out and the house was quiet again, Irene sat outside on the verandah with Rudy, Yvonne and Jeff while Yvonne's husband Mike, a teacher at an American university, stayed inside with their children.

'Your father was a good man.' In speaking to her daughter Yvonne, Irene used the same phrase as the brash New Yorker had expressed a couple of hours earlier but her tone could not have been more different. Yvonne was exhausted and lay back in a chair with her eyes closed. The two men were also tired, having consumed so much beer. But Irene seemed to grow fresher as the sun went down, and the others listened respectfully as she carried on talking about Lionel.

'He was, as they say, larger than life,' she said. 'I guess death was the only thing he couldn't talk himself out of. He was such a special man, so alive, it's just so hard to think that he won't ever burst through that door again in that way of his.

'You know, a few years back, there was a fire at the stables, at Knutsford. Not a big blaze or anything but enough for everyone to run off and call the fire brigade. Yet Lionel and one of the trainers went back in for a pair of horses that were trapped in there. Lionel didn't tell me about that; the chief fireman did.

'It's funny, we were talking about you children only last week. Wondering what you were doing and about when we could all get together again. Who would have thought you would be sitting here in person a few days on and him gone? God, he loved you two. He was always so proud. "Have you heard what my son's been doing? In London?" he would say. Or, "Have you heard my daughter play the piano? She can make grown men cry."

'He may not have been a religious man, but Friday nights were always special, I lit candles when you were kids.'

'That's when we were allowed to read comics and listen to music,' said Rudy, smiling at the memory.

'And sweets,' added Irene. 'Friday evening was the one time in the week you were allowed sweets. Once, when you were little, Yvonne, I was out with you on Orange Street and – oh I can remember it so clearly – I stopped to chat with a friend of mine who had her little daughter with her and when they were gone you said to me, "Mummy, did you see that naughty girl? She was eating a chocolate bar and it isn't even Friday."'

Amid the laughter at this recollection, Irene leaned forward and tapped Jeff on the knee. 'I know you and Lionel weren't quite so thick lately as in the old days, but you're going to miss him, aren't you.'

'Yes, I'm really going to miss him,' Jeff affirmed. 'He set me up here. It's like being orphaned. Lionel was the only one in Jamaica I could fall back on. Together with you, of course.'

Irene was still leaning forward. Tears began to push their way down her face. 'Oh, look at me,' she said, and then wept silently into her hands.

Jeff could not bear the silence and began to talk compulsively. 'You know, this is only the second funeral I can remember going to in Jamaica,' he said. 'The other one was when that young boy died, the little chap who used to come and help in the shop after school. Clyde. You remember he drowned? I've never seen such crying as at that funeral. A whole line of ladies in brightly coloured hats were weeping together so loudly I thought one of them would burst. I was standing next to one sweet old dear. "You know what crying is," she says to me, these other women still sobbing away. "Crying is the one time we get to wash in the water from the river of love that flows through us all." I'll never forget that.'

After another moment or two of silence, Jeff stood up and broke open another bottle of Red Stripe for himself. 'Yes, I certainly am going to miss old Lionel,' he said. And then, stroking Irene's hair, 'There is nobody who can replace him.'

Just then, Yvonne's husband, Mike, appeared on the verandah. 'The children are asleep,' he announced and walked over to his wife and embraced her.

'Goodnight, my children,' Irene said as Mike released Yvonne, allowing her to turn towards her mother. And Yvonne and Rudy each gave Irene an arm to help her from her chair. 'Goodnight, my sweet children,' she said, stroking both of their faces.

Twenty-five

Benny and especially Bertha Pomeranski were thrilled and proud when their son Simon was accepted as an undergraduate at Cambridge University. Bertha would have liked him to study something practical or vocational, with both prestige and outstanding career prospects attached – law, for example, or medicine – and her enthusiasm was somewhat dented when she finally was forced to accept that he was going to do three years of English (she was also concerned that, as he was to become a member of *Trinity* College, he might be prey to Christian missionary activity).

'You already know English, Simon,' Bertha said to her son, reasonably enough. 'Everybody knows English. Your father and I can both speak it quite well, as can you. Surely you don't need to be taught something so basic at your age.'

'I'm reading English Literature, Ma. I'll be studying the work of the great authors.'

'Surely you can read what you want, whenever you want, now. You read enough books as it is – as do I. So does your father. He reads all kinds of stuff, Mickey Spillane, *Exodus* by Leon Uris, and grander stuff like, I don't know… Dickens. So what's to learn? You don't need to be taught how to read! Dad never went to university and, apart from Mr Wagman and that other teacher at his school who sounds like he was a bit of a *schmerel*, nobody needed to teach him. So what can they teach you?'

'There's a lot more to it than school. In a sense, I *will* be learning how to read. Not the meaning of individual words, or grammar, but how authors contribute to civilisation, to culture. And I'll be reading plays, which I am really looking forward to.'

'What, do you want to be an actor?'

'Possibly.'

'You'll take years to earn a proper living and even then it's not guaranteed. Lots of actors end up earning a few bob as waiters or waitresses – if they're lucky. Whereas if you were a doctor or a lawyer, you'd be earning right from the start. Your job will be waiting for you. You won't have to go through all that interview business and spend hours on end trying to work out what job you want – or can get.'

'*Ma*! Dad and I have spent many months, *years* even, trying to get it into your head that in order to do medicine you must have studied biology and chemistry, and done brilliantly in both of them. The last time I shut my science exercise book was three years ago, with great relief and pleasure. And law... *nah*, not for me,' he said after a pause.

'I love English.' Simon continued trying to convince his mother of the wisdom of taking his chosen path. 'Just imagine the privilege of studying a subject you love with the best teachers – which will mean I'll work hard at it.'

'Well, you'd work hard at whatever you did.'

In truth, in contrast to her earlier ambitions for her son, Bertha was now inwardly worried that he might turn his back on his parents once he found himself in the rarefied atmosphere of Cambridge.

Benny's attitude was much more encouraging. And he was more ready to show his pride. 'Guess what! Simon's got into Cambridge,' he boasted to Estelle. 'Hey, Spanish,' he called out when he saw Joe Pelovsky one afternoon coming along Excelsior's Fourth Avenue towards Pomeranski Gowns. 'What do you think of my boy, Simon? He's got himself into Cambridge University.'

'*Mazeltov*,' said Spanish Joe, beaming. 'He must have Bertha's brains,' he added, smirking.

'Yeah, you're right. Her brains and my looks.'

Bertha's utilitarian attitude towards her son's education had eased significantly by the end of his first year at Trinity when he appeared in a college production of *Hamlet*, in which he undertook the role of the First Player in a band of strolling theatricals.

As such, Simon had to grapple with a daunting speech about the brutal and merciless murder of Hecuba's husband Priam by Pyrrhus in the Trojan War. The First Player's speech triggers another, much more famous one by Prince Hamlet, expressing amazement at the art of acting and the unique dedication of actors, whose job is to pretend to be someone else.

Neither Bertha nor Benny went to Cambridge to see Simon in the Trinity *Hamlet*, but Bertha listened to him rehearse that key Pyrrhus speech over and over throughout a weekend at home, and was profoundly impressed by her son's meticulous intensity. And when, on graduating two years later, Simon and a couple of other Cambridge thespians joined a small touring theatre company, The Scene Stealers – with the very opposite of a 'guaranteed' income – Bertha gave him her full support. She became a regular in the Scene Stealers' audience whenever they reached London, *kvelling* with pride for her son, however indifferent she felt towards the play she happened to be watching.

Eventually, Simon Pomeranski took on directing duties with the Scene Stealers and enjoyed some success at the Edinburgh Festival and London fringes. And, when a new actress, Marina Lawson, whom he had slightly known at Cambridge, auditioned and was taken on by the company, she and Simon soon found themselves in tune offstage as well as on. Their marriage, three years later, coincided with Simon's appointment as vice-principal of the Blackheath Drama School in South London.

It was always his ambition, fuelled by nostalgia for that Cambridge *Hamlet*, to put on a production of the play but it wasn't until a young actor called Edward Lowden, the nephew of an actress at the Royal Shakespeare Company, came to Blackheath that Simon knew he had someone who could inhabit Shakespeare's most celebrated character.

All this time, Simon Pomeranski retained his fascination with his father's Astorian world, though now somewhat at arm's length. His boyhood wish to become involved in even their 'below-the-counter' activities dwindled in his undergraduate days but he still went occasionally to revisit Excelsior Arcade. 'It is true *theatre*,' he would later claim to Marina and his colleagues.

In their young days, Simon and Marina's sons, Will and Jonathan, loved being taken for walks around Brixton Market. And their grandparents loved it even more when Marina and Simon brought the boys into Pomeranski Gowns, where Benny put on women's hats to make them laugh and then placed them on the boys' heads and showed them how they looked in the shop's full-length mirror.

Simon even told them stories about Spanish Joe, Joey the Boxer and 'Naughty Little Jack'. And when directing Edward Lowden, Simon kept that Brixton ethos firmly in mind. His vision for Edward's performance centred on Hamlet's outcry against his uncle, the 'bloody, bawdy villain! Remorseless, treachery, lecherous, kindless villain! O vengeance!'

So taken with Edward Lowden's verse-speaking skills, stage presence and astonishing versatility (Edward would later follow his aunt into the Royal Shakespeare Company) was Simon that he exploited these and other of Lowden's qualities by adapting Robert Louis Stevenson's *Treasure Island* for the stage with Lowden as the redoubtable one-legged pirate, Long John Silver. This time, the core speech that Simon focused on was one he wrote himself, again with its speaker raging about vengeance:

'If any there be that defy me, or deform me more than I am deformed – which is little – then I shall show thee what terrible pains can follow from defiance and deformity. And do not expect mercy. Though I be not full quota for dancing, be sure that I shall enjoy the music of thy bloody suffering!'

To a significant extent, for his piratical play and its principal character, Simon Pomeranski drew on Samuel Golub, Sam the Stick, the Astorian example of a 'one-legged' individual who carried 'defiance and deformity' in his body, and vengeance in his heart. But, while soaking up the acclaim with which his *Treasure Island* was showered, Simon Pomeranski had no idea that fictional similarity was about to be extended into the realms of fearful, real-life coincidence And that, within days of the opening performances of both his *Hamlet* and his *Treasure Island*, the last act of a story of overweening villainy would be played out, on a stage beyond theatre, within the everlasting drama that was Brixton.

Twenty-six

Getting to see Little Jack was a bit like getting an audience with the Pope. 'What's troubling you, Sammy,' his holiness asked when Sam finally got through to him on the telephone after several days of trying. 'How can I help?'

'It's private, Jack. It's about my mother. I'm worried. I need help. But I have to talk to you in private.'

'Sure, sure, little man. Business not so good, eh? I never thought you would seek *my* guidance, though you obviously could do with it. Come and see me at the club on Thursday afternoon.'

This was what Sam the Stick had been banking on. Thursday was the day Little Jack's foot soldiers were around, lounging in the Jax bar before the regular weekly meetings. Sam knew that all the nearest car-parking places would be taken by the gang and that he would have to park a few streets away, not so close to the river. That suited him fine.

So, on that next Thursday, he duly parked his disability-adapted Rover a considerable distance from the Jax club and then walked for a mile before forcing open a gate into an alley that led to the back of the building.

At the end of the alley, some way beyond the club's rear tradesmen's entrance, was a dilapidated car repair shop that had been closed for months. Inside it, a week or so earlier, Sam had hidden a collapsible ladder. He now entered the shop using the key to the new padlock that he'd fitted when he'd gone there with the ladder. He removed the ladder, carried it back along the deserted alley and used it to get to the top of the jazz club's fire escape from the opposite direction to the steps that led down.

From there, Sam made his way into the first floor of the building, closed the fire escape door behind him and went through a door to his right, which led into the lavatory. As he entered, he could hear music coming from Little Jack's office. Jack was constantly buying himself records and playing them at high volume. Sam silently prayed that Jack was in his office at that moment and not using the lavatory. He pushed the inner door open, slowly and carefully. To his relief, the lavatory was empty. There were two more lavatories downstairs and Sam knew it was unlikely that any of Little Jack's boys would come upstairs to this one, situated in the boss's domain.

There was a second door in the lavatory, which led to a landing. Sam went out silently through this door. All that now lay between him and Little Jack Lewis's office along the landing was an opening on to a narrow staircase leading to the downstairs entrance area.

Sam had to get past the top of the stairs without anyone seeing him from below. He peered round the landing wall at the top of the stairs and saw nobody. In a second, he was across and outside Little Jack's office. He uttered a further prayer for Jack to be in there alone. Then he knocked on the door and went in without waiting to be asked. Little Jack had his feet up on the desk. He was listening to Louis Armstrong playing and singing George Gershwin's 'I Was Doing All Right'.

'Sammy! How'd you manage to get in unannounced, you cheeky *kalikah*? And you're early. What *chutzpah!*' Jack brought down his feet from the desk and extended a hand towards Sam. 'How are you, you little *lobbes*. Benny let you down, I suppose? I'm not that surprised. I didn't hear you knock. I must have had the gramophone on too loud. Hang on a minute, I'll turn it down.'

Sam held up his hand. 'No,' he said. 'Not yet. I love this. Satchmo has to be listened to loud.'

'You're right there, Sammy boy. Well, well, I didn't know you were such a man of taste.'

'Sure. In fact, it could be a little louder. Like having that unmistakable voice and that magic trumpet play for you in your own room, don't you think?'

'Okay,' said Little Jack. If you can take it, I certainly can. Turn it up.'

'Oh, I couldn't touch your posh gramophone, Jack. I'd be afraid I'd break something.'

'What are you talking about? It's dead easy. Let me show you the volume switch. Look, *kalikah*, I'll do it. I dunno, I thought you were just crippled in your leg, not in your hands and your brains also.'

This remark, along with being called a *kalikah* – a cripple – made it easier for Sam to do what he had come to do. And when Little Jack Lewis leaned towards the record player to turn up the sound of Louis Armstrong – *Had no cause to complain / Life was as sweet as apple pie* – Sammy Golub, like a conjurer, in one nimble movement, produced a small derringer pistol from his pocket and jammed it precisely where he had painstakingly planned to – into a point on Little Jack's temple – and pulled the trigger.

The sound was absorbed, along with Armstrong's sweetly rough voice, into the music's brassy background. Sam took a swift step backwards to avoid the blood that pumped out from one of those human beings who, in Sam the Stick's philosophy, 'deserved it', as Jack Lewis slumped to the floor.

Little Jack hadn't even made it as far as his prized gramophone. Sam walked in a wide arc around him and, with a gloved hand, turned up the volume on the showily expensive disc player. 'As I said,' he whispered to himself, 'I like it even louder.' And he placed the derringer exactly as he had rehearsed in order to make it look like suicide.

> *Never noticed the rain*
> *Till you came by*

It took Sam about fifteen minutes to get back the way he came, lock away the ladder, retrace his steps down the alleyway, take off the gloves he was wearing, put them in his car, and walk a more orthodox route to the front of the club.

When he arrived, he was relieved to see that nobody had yet noticed anything. He couldn't believe his luck as he exchanged greetings with people at the bar. 'Watcha, Sam,' said the first familiar face, that of Eddie Lawrence, the Jax club manager, a likeable fifty-year-old Jamaican who, despite being on Little Jack Lewis's payroll, managed to be on friendly terms with the Astorian boys – and who was also bright, friendly and quite a hot clarinet 'blower'. 'How goes it?' Eddie enquired. 'What are you up to?'

'I've got a meeting with Little Jack. Mum's bills,' Sam replied credibly. 'She's having a tough time now Dad's dead. Jack said he'd help – you know.'

'Right you are,' said Eddie. 'What time you seeing him?'

'Soon,' Sam shrugged. 'I'm a little early. I think I'll have a drink.'

'Well, he should be down before long. The music's stopped upstairs. It was belting out a few minutes ago.'

Not that it was quiet downstairs. A tape behind the bar was playing modern jazz as a background to the laughter and chatter among the assembled villains, hangers-on and genuine customers. Sam ordered a Scotch. While Tony the barman was getting it, a loud, heavily built man with a self-satisfied swagger, pin-striped suit and a rough London accent shouted impatiently at Tony: 'Eh, mate, can we have a couple of beers here pronto? We're really thirsty.'

'He's just getting my drink,' said Sam amiably to the man, whom he'd never seen before.

'Who asked you?' the big man snapped back.

Eddie Lawrence hastily intervened to try to prevent an unpleasant scene: 'Hey Bill, go easy,' he said, 'this is Sam – Sam the Stick. He's okay. He's harmless. A friend. One of us. Bill-Sam, Sam-Big Bill.'

Even though he had understandably taken against the bulky stranger (who, it turned out, was an ex-cop friend of Little Jack Lewis, whom he'd met through some shady property dealings and a shared love of jazz) and did not like being called 'harmless', even by the sunny-countenanced Eddie Lawrence, Sam, amazed at how relaxed he felt, was nevertheless ready to shake hands.

Not so, Big Bill, however. 'He may be harmless,' he snorted, 'but that doesn't mean he can poke his nose in where it's not wanted.'

Samuel Golub was having quite a day. Those who witnessed it described the manner in which he lashed the inflated ex-copper's face, with his trusty stick, as a mixture of breathtaking power and speed. 'Sheer choreography' was the phrase used by one of the more poetically inclined onlookers. Big Bill himself was in no real position to describe it as he had crashed, face-down and semi-conscious, to the floor.

'Now,' announced Sam, his nerve still holding remarkably well, 'can somebody please tell Little Jack I'm here?'

'Yeah, sure, Sam,' said Eddie, as others tended to Sam's victim. 'I'll go up to the office and tell him. He's expecting you, isn't he?'

'Yes,' said Sam, 'we spoke very recently.'

Twenty-seven

Jeff Calloway strolled down Orange Street for the last time. It was Sunday morning, cool and early, and there weren't too many people about. Not that it mattered. He had already said his farewells to the people; now he wanted to bid goodbye to the place itself. All the old haunts. And Orange Street was the oldest haunt of all.

Even though he was as much at home as he could be in Jamaica after so many years and had made more than enough money to lead a comfortable life, his long-suppressed wish to end his days on the west coast of Ireland began to re-emerge into his thoughts. He had plenty more years in him, and felt he would be able to calm down, adapt and acclimatise to Ireland as he'd adapted and acclimatised years earlier to Jamaica.

West Cork, Clare and sometimes Mayo were where he had spent his childhood holidays and where he had felt the closest to nature. It was a feeling that he believed had lodged in his heart and would come back to inspire him now, deep into his adulthood, and indeed for eternity. And, he also believed, it was time to leave Jamaica. 'A peaceful farewell,' he told himself, 'with regret, with gratitude, but my work, my time here, is done.'

He came to a stop outside Solomons's store, long under different ownership, and, looking through the window, smiled and sighed. This was where it had all begun. He had established himself relatively quickly within a certain segment of Kingston society. But then, he did enjoy the best of beginnings. From the very moment of his arrival, Lionel Solomons had taken him under his wing and, when Lionel died in 1972, it felt to Jeff that he had lost not so much a father figure, but more an inspirational spirit.

Lionel had been amused by Jeff's keenness to succeed in the early days and did not interfere with him except occasionally to tell him to slow down: 'You are going a little too fast, Jeff my boy. Take it easy.'

Eventually, Jeff did slow down, but not principally as a result of Lionel's urging. It all stemmed from the night he came out of the Sombrero club with Marie Valentine when, at the precise moment that he was thinking about how much he loved this woman who was so unlike any other woman he had met in the Sombrero, or anywhere else, and was about to tell her as much, a mysterious man – who had never been identified – opened his car door and fired a shot at them.

Now, years on, Jeff was wondering if he had done the right thing by insisting the police drop the case and call off their searches. They had quickly ruled out the young white-suited lover boy Jeff had ejected from the Sombrero. 'No,' the chief detective said. 'He doesn't do guns – and he had an alibi.' More than anything, the incident had a sobering effect on Jeff – as did Marie, whom he married a few months later.

Thereafter, he worked hard in Solomons's store and concentrated his energies on succeeding in business, buying up real estate as well as extending his own network of contacts in the textile business, which Lionel had encouraged him to do within days of employing him at the store. 'You can be more useful to me as an independent,' Lionel had told him. 'And, besides,' he'd said with a full and friendly laugh, 'the more independent you are, the less I have to pay you!'

In Lionel's endorsement and the fact that his skin was coffee-coloured, slightly darkened by the West Indian sun but not black, Jeff had two important advantages in the Jamaica of that time. After five years, he was happily married, doing well in the property trade and living in his own house on Seaview Avenue, close to Liguanea.

But one day, when he was taking Marie for a spin in a smart, fast car that he had borrowed from a friend, he collided with a bus. The car's passenger side took the full impact and Marie died instantly. She was three months' pregnant and the baby was lost. Though unharmed physically, mentally Jeff was crushed.

He went back to stay with Lionel and Irene, who helped him gradually to feel human again. He sold his house and bought a smaller property closer to the Solomonses. He took less and less interest in the shadier side of life and stayed away from the parties at Lionel's house, where the visiting 'dignitaries' could include racketeers from New York, Cuba and Miami, as well as film producers, politicians, sportsmen and semi-official visitors from Jewish communities in London, Los Angeles or Toronto.

He became obsessed with being respectable. After a year or so, he married again. His bride was the daughter of one of Irene's card-playing ladies. But the memory of Marie was too insistently present in his mind and the second marriage lasted only two-and-a-half years. Nevertheless, he remained an active member of the Kingston business community. He took his clients to cricket matches at Sabina Park. He even went to church a few times.

Occasionally, he became a little restless. He countered this by getting together with some of his old cronies periodically at the cricket and tennis club or for lunch at the Myrtle Bay Hotel by the harbour. Sometimes he would swim in the pool there, a privilege that would have been denied him had his skin been darker.

And he enjoyed driving and working on cars. For a long time, he had a Hillman Minx and then, in the 1960s, he bought a white Thunderbird upon which he lavished a great deal of attention. He kept it for years, hardly driving it at all after a while, but still ensuring it was always immaculate and shining.

He cut down on the booze, though he continued to enjoy the odd cooling nip of Red Stripe. Around him, life in Kingston changed and he had no more desire to be in the thick of it. One day, a black man dived into the Myrtle Bank Hotel pool and the old, rigid colonial foundations were shaken. Jeff's superior status, derived from his lighter skin pigmentation, was no longer secure. The black man's day had arrived at last. Jamaica had come of age.

As time and friends passed, Jeff missed all the old faces. The Jewish guys at the Knutsford Park track with their expressive gestures that mingled appreciation and exasperation. The 'dudes' he drank with into the early hours at the Sombrero in the days before Marie came along. As for the 'mischief', the new currency was drugs, and the new young gangs involved in it were reckless and wild, lacking Lionel's Raffles-like style and decorum, and cruder than Jeff's own audacious smuggling and clinically handled persuasions and paybacks. He was glad to be out of it.

He quietly built up his business and began to take a back seat, handing the reins to others. Then, one day, he was tinkering underneath his latest car, a Chevrolet, when he couldn't get up from the ground. He had no strength in his limbs and the pain in his head was so bad he couldn't see. 'I've got to leave,' he told himself, when the doctor informed him that if he didn't retire he could be dead in a few months.

His decision to leave Jamaica became firmer with each new day. Not only had Lionel's death left him missing the old boy and mourning him for years but, one day, Irene announced she was leaving to join Yvonne in America. It was this that finally and conclusively persuaded him to sell up and leave Jamaica. Even if Ireland turned out to be an unrealistic fantasy, his longstanding business colleague, correspondent and friend, Benny Pomeranski, had said he could find him a place in London or maybe in the Kent countryside.

And now Jeffrey Johnson Calloway was making his last rounds. Peering in through the windows of Solomons's at the seat in front of the counter where Lionel used to hold court while Irene dashed around offering glasses of lemon tea in between serving customers, he found it hard to tear himself away. Placing his face right against the window glass, he could almost see Lionel, extravagantly dressed in silk cravat and Bond Street shirt, white suit and handmade shoes, waving his hands, laughing and declaiming to an assortment of rapt listeners.

Part Two

One

Sing Sing Prison, New York, 18 June 1953

Dearest Sweethearts, my most precious children.

Only this morning it looked like we might be together again after all. Now that this cannot be, I want so much for you to know all that I have come to know... Eventually... you must come to believe that life is worth the living. Be comforted that even now, with the end of ours slowly approaching, we know this with a conviction that defeats the executioner! Your lives must teach you, too, that good cannot really flourish in the midst of evil; that freedom and all the things that go to make up a truly satisfying and worthwhile life, must sometimes be purchased very dearly... Your Daddy, who is with me in the last momentous hours, sends his heart and all the love that is in it for his dearest boys. Always remember that we were innocent and could not wrong our conscience. We press you close and kiss you with all our strength.

Lovingly, Daddy and Mommy, Julie, Ethel

LETTER FROM ETHEL AND JULIUS ROSENBERG TO THEIR SONS, AGED TEN AND SIX, WRITTEN THE DAY BEFORE THEY WERE BOTH EXECUTED FOR PASSING AMERICAN ATOMIC SECRETS TO THE SOVIET UNION. THE TIMING OF THEIR EXECUTION, ON 19 JUNE 1953, HAD BEEN BROUGHT FORWARD TO AVOID IT TAKING PLACE ON THE JEWISH SABBATH. *NEW YORK TIMES*, JUNE 1953

In the weeks following Benny Pomeranski's death, his widow Bertha and son Simon spent many hours going through his belongings. One day, Simon took down a dust-covered, long-unused suitcase from the top of an archaic wardrobe in a corner of his parents', and latterly just his mother's, bedroom.

He laid the suitcase across the bed and pulled out a box of paper tissues from a drawer in his late father's bedside table – which still smelled faintly of the brand of cologne Benny had used from before he was married right up to his last days. Simon dampened a couple of the tissues with a little water to wipe the top of the suitcase before opening it. Inside, he found two silk ties; a white shirt still in the unopened pack in which it had been purchased sixteen years earlier; a pair of torn woollen gloves; and a large cardboard folder.

The folder, in turn, contained a batch of black-and-white photographs held together by a large rubber band; a small bundle of love letters that had passed between the young Bombardier Benjamin Pomeranski and the then Bertha Yanovsky, each letter, from either party, addressed to 'My darling B' and signed by 'Your ever-loving B'; and two thick lined exercise books, labelled respectively, 'Journal' and 'Journal Two', their single stream of contents flowing from the end of the former into the start of the latter.

Bertha was out of the flat when Simon made this discovery, and he took the opportunity to read some of Bertha and Benny's wartime love letters, an emotional experience that seemed to annihilate the distance of years, attitudes and misunderstanding that he had previously perceived between his parents and himself.

Having carefully placed the letters in Bertha's dressing-table drawer so that she could read them later, Simon turned his attention to the two journals. These were filled with numerous observations, opinions, confessions, revelations, reflections and routine diary entries, all handwritten by Benny Pomeranski. They dated from the beginning of his affair with Estelle Davis and continued, on and off, into the last days of his life.

Benny had also pasted into his long-running journal various newspaper cuttings, to which he often added a concise comment.

Alongside one press photograph – that of the athlete Roger Bannister, exhausted after having just become the first man to run a mile in under four minutes, beating by two seconds the previous world record which had stood for nine years – Benny had written: 'Is there any limit to man's progress into the "impossible"?'

Underneath a cutting about Julius and Ethel Rosenberg, an American Jewish married couple who were sent to the electric chair for passing information about US atomic-bomb capability to the Soviet Union, Benny had written: 'Did they have to be killed?' He'd gone on to speculate at some length on the lives and motives of the Rosenbergs. Were they naïve idealists? Was President Dwight D. Eisenhower right to say that the information they gave away could have led to many thousands of American deaths and to insist on their execution? Benny Pomeranski closed his personal peroration with a brief, factual and poignant statement: 'Pleas for clemency were rejected and the Rosenbergs' two young children were orphaned in just over a quarter of an hour of controlled electrocution.'

In a lighter but still enthusiastic set of entries, Benny's journal revealed him welcoming the new sounds of rock'n'roll and other transformative forms of popular music that mushroomed in the 1950s and 1960s. This did not at all encroach upon his devotion to Ellington, Basie, Armstrong, Sinatra, Fitzgerald and various other purveyors of jazz and the Great American Songbook, or his love for Yiddish music and Hebrew cantorial singing inherited from his father. And he was happy to allow his record collection being mingled with his son's at the end of the 1960s. 'We're all shook up' – a reference to an Elvis Presley song from a decade earlier – was how he summed up that particular concession.

Just over three decades later, that same son, Simon Pomeranski, perusing two old exercise books, was transfixed by his father's outpourings, both serious and frivolous. This was partly because they could be construed as a valediction, a father's farewell to his son, and partly, certainly in Simon's eyes, as a vindication of his long-held romantic view of Benny's connection to Pomeranski Gowns, Excelsior Arcade, the Brixton Empress – and the Astorians.

At his first sight of Benny's notes in the journal, Simon feared they would reveal what would have been an unwelcome and demoralising discovery – that Benny, Sam, Spanish Joe and the others were essentially nasty, anti-social villains rather than the lovable rogues of his imaginings. But, to his great relief, far from being the self-serving screed of a petty-minded, boastful or defensive criminal, Benny's many journal reflections, particularly the later ones issuing from a dying man settling his account with mortality – to which Simon turned first – were free from malice or self-aggrandisement. Taken together, they formed a kind of memoir, a retrospective, personal credo of an exceptional individual.

This is not to say that Benny the Fixer was unconcerned to justify his actions, whether lawful or not. 'When I came home from the war,' he wrote, 'I wanted to be the king of the castle, but with Bertha's down-to-earth attitude as my example I came to see that you can't wish away reality.

'I have always challenged authority, and refused to be exploited by, or play the games of, high-ranking, rich and privileged people who set the rules in their own interests. In all this, I don't think I have overstepped the mark too often. And, while it's bit of a laugh, I feel it's a little bit ironic to be called a *macher*, a big shot.

'And if I'm a "fixer", okay, but it's just that I know what can be done in certain situations, and what can't, and what should be done and what shouldn't. Not in a moral or religious way but I try to be fair and make the most of whatever talents I happened to be born with. A conventional, conforming social life, involving unquestioning acceptance of whatever you are given or told, was never for me. I've always needed to reach beyond the facade and seek excitement. I've chosen life!

'The Farringdon operation was a symbol of what I have gone about doing. Nobody was hurt or even out of pocket. I relieved a small group of my so-called Jewish brethren of some ill-gotten gains and I hope, as a result of the shock we gave them, that the members of that particular cosy clan can now stop raking through masses of biblical minutiae that they can bend and twist to justify their actions.

'But I hope they keep on giving to charity and generally trying to do good, as I have tried to do ever since I helped Sammy Golub trash Hughie Cartwright's shop when we left the East End behind. I still feel ashamed about what we did that day but I did at least keep Sam from committing even more mayhem.

'I'm very proud that my son Simon went to Cambridge University, though I believe I've learned more than he has about life, on the outside. Real life, where not everyone you meet is intelligent, friendly and understanding. It's important to know how to handle the bastards and the morons, and the things that go wrong. The setbacks. The paybacks.

'But Simon's all right. As well as a brain and a bright, clever wife and children, he also has talent. His Treasure Island play is brilliant, funny, thrilling, and even clairvoyant. That marvellously *creative* achievement by my beloved son uncannily mirrored a marvellously *destructive* achievement by my oldest friend, Sam the Stick, the Jewish Long John Silver!

'Growing up, I had very little formal education but I was very inquisitive. When I was a kid, I was always throwing sceptical questions at my parents about their Judaism. Why did they allow only kosher food in the house but happily eat bacon sandwiches at Cath's Café in Excelsior Arcade? Why did my mother fast on Yom Kippur but not my father, while both of them told me I was perfectly free not to fast, if that's what I wanted? My ungrateful response to their indulgence of me and my brothers, and of each other, was to call them hypocrites. *Hypocrites*! My poor, kind, hard-working parents. What a precocious brat I must have been.

'But when I got married and set up home, I missed my mother's lighting of the candles and her serving up of chicken soup on Friday nights. And I came to understand my parents' way of life. "Empathy", I believe, is the word. And I quickly came to appreciate them. Bertha and I have lived in much the same way. Keeping the rituals: eating matzos at Passover; going to *shul* on Jewish festivals despite not believing in the religious message; having our son circumcised and thirteen years later throwing a nice little bar mitzvah party for him. I'd thought I was different but I was the same all along.

'But I still want to challenge the teachings, the rules. The laws. So many of them are relevant exclusively to an ancient, primitive desert way of life, without electricity, refrigeration, modern medicine, hygiene or a healthy water supply. Notwithstanding the unquestioning obedience of very religious people to every little law – those who are sometimes called the "real Jews" – I think that curiosity, trying to get to the bottom of things, not always accepting things at face value – or biblical value – is a Jewish trait.

'I suppose you could say that my true religion is hypocrisy. I've certainly broken most of the Ten Commandments in my time.

'All the same, being Jewish is what makes me tick. You don't have to be a synagogue-goer for that to be the case. It's all sorts of things. It's those old traditions and customs that keep the whole glorious show on the road. It's family. Jewish stories and storytellers, and jokes and joke-tellers. Jewish food. Belonging to a group, which is why I set up the Astorians. Sitting round a table talking, agreeing, *disagreeing,* and laughing with friends or family. Jews argue and ask questions; they want to know more, always to learn. We read. We write. We listen to music. We play music. We dance at weddings. We're sentimental. Sensual. Passionate. Committed, mostly to just causes but sometimes, like the Rosenbergs, to a wrong one.

'We give to charity. We hug. We kiss. We even kiss our texts, sacred and profane. (In my case, there are some "profane" writings that I consider sacred, like the novel "Heart of Darkness", by Joseph Conrad, first recommended to me by my not really Spanish but definitely queer friend "Spanish" Joe Pelovsky. And "Great Expectations", by Charles Dickens, of which my father gave me his own copy. Or the poetry of that *yiddified,* Jew-hating, genius, T. S. Eliot. And of course the even greater poetry by an even greater genius, William Shakespeare.)

'Jews think getting an education, even if you get it completely through your own efforts, is the best bloody thing in the world. We respect clever people, Jewish or not; and have *rachmanes,* compassion, for dunces, Jewish or not.

'And, for me... revering the "idolatry" of the paintings of Rembrandt; succumbing to the forbidden purity of so many female voices (not just Estelle's but Ella Fitzgerald's, Birgit Nilsson's and even Mahalia Jackson singing the Christian "Lord's Prayer"); eating the occasional bacon sandwich; or driving my car on the Sabbath... does not diminish any of it.'

Two

A last-minute plea to save Ruth Ellis from the gallows on Wednesday was made yesterday to Major Gwilym Lloyd George, the Home Secretary. He is spending an anxious weekend pondering, away from Whitehall officials' assistance, this plea and other petitions – 10,000 more signatures asking for a reprieve were delivered last evening. The new appeal, sent to the Home Office by Ruth Ellis's solicitor, Mr John Bickford, accompanied dramatic new information concerning her life. It was this: she was a sick woman at the time she shot her lover, racing motorist David Blakely. She was a self-confessed alcoholic. And only a few days before the shooting on Easter Sunday, she was a mother-to-be. But a miscarriage intervened.

Reynolds News, July 1955

As he read page after page of Benny's familiar, neat and looped handwriting, Simon was completely absorbed. He recognised the emotional, self-taught, book-loving and *chutzpahdik* father he loved. But he could not remember any serious conversations with him about the deeper and intimate subjects that ran through his journal. Nor about human relationships of any kind. And now, a mere few weeks after Benny the Macher's death, his son Simon found himself face-to-face – in an accidentally discovered pair of exercise books hidden in a suitcase on top of a redundant wardrobe – not only with his father's impassioned assertion of his Jewish identity, but also with a sensual counterpoint to the revelations Bertha had delivered in the back seat of the hearse departing from the cemetery after Benny's funeral.

'Estie and I separated today,' was how Benny began the pertinent paragraph. 'I have set her free. And I must return to reality. I cannot face the possibility of so much sadness, so much sweetness turning sour.

'When we were together in Brighton that first time, there were moments which were completely perfect. Not just in making love, but in everything around us. Watching the sunrise with her. The majestic, living colours of the sunset. The cries of the gulls heralding the sound of the sea. Even the noises of the hotel breakfast being prepared, the waiter whistling jolly tunes. The fragrance and colours of our room. The cheap paintings on the wall. The softness of the pillows. The bed. The little china ornaments. The nearness of her, her touch, her smile, her smell. The way we fitted so neatly into each other's arms. The laughter, which will always stay with me. Walking along the seashore. The knowledge that she felt exactly the same as I did.

'But eventually the tide comes in. The darkness. Always. Not just in Brighton. And not just by the sea.'

This recollection came to an end at the foot of a page and, when Simon turned over, the next page was blank except for, in the left-hand lower corner, without any comment, a short, just-legible, unsigned, untitled poem:

> She is my love,
> Reflected in my eyes
> Imprinted on my brain
> Where I am in disguise
>
> She is my love,
> And sings above the noise
> And me, I am merely
> The echo of her voice

She is my love,
And though she pours my wine
And I blend into her
She never can be mine

Quirkily, because of the voracious press interest, almost as many words were spent on Ruth Ellis in Benny's journal (though mainly in the pasted-in press cuttings) as on Estelle Davis. He met Ruth only a few times and never had what could be described as a proper conversation with her. Their first encounter was at Estelle's singing debut at the Sly Fox's first Cabaret Night and there were just two or three later occasions at the Sly Fox.

Within a lengthy description, in his journal notes, of hearing Estelle sing for the first time ('her looks exactly matched her voice... this song can never have sounded more seductive'), Benny Pomeranski recalled that, sitting at the table before the show started, Ruth Ellis's boyfriend, David Blakely – the man she later shot dead outside the Magdala pub in Hampstead, for which she would become forever known as 'the last woman to be hanged in Britain' – had talked over Ruth's attempts at conversation and groaned when she did manage to 'get a word in edgeways to break up his tedious motor-racing monologue'.

Three weeks into Estelle's singing stint, Ruth Ellis left the Sly Fox but still came back each week to hear Estelle sing. They continued to see each other and became close friends. Estelle went for a drink with Ruth at the Bull and Bush pub in Hampstead in March 1955, just a couple of weeks or so before the shooting took place.

After the initial shock at having heard about Ruth's arrest and the killing of David Blakely, Estelle appeared to steel herself against prolonging her own distress. She visited Ruth twice in Holloway Prison. The first time, she came away upset and tearful and sank into Benny's arms when he collected her afterwards. 'People don't realise what she has had to put up with,' she said. 'Any woman would understand. That bastard got what he deserved. She should not be facing a possible death sentence.'

But, after her second visit, Estelle announced that, while she would continue to write to Ruth, she would not be visiting her again. 'She doesn't care if she lives or dies,' Estelle told Benny. 'Sadly, this is one you can't fix, Mr Fixer.'

Benny did, however, devote a considerable amount of space to Estelle's friend in his private journal – pondering how the shooting of David Blakely came about and what it said about the fragility of personal relationships, and the persons in them.

'How could Estelle have cut off her sadness about Ruth so easily, not even speaking about her any more?' he wrote. 'Is it a strategy for coping with the possibility of her friend's execution? She clearly does not want me to bring up the subject.'

But he did bring it up, just after they had both signed one of the petitions demanding leniency for Ruth. This was brought to them one afternoon by Amelia Constant, the mother of Harvey Constant of Excelsior Records, as they sat in the Astoria café. And, while Estelle and Benny pushed aside their coffee cups and added their signatures to the bulky document before them on the table, Amelia disclosed to them the astonishing information that her husband, Milton Constant, Harvey's father, had employed Ruth Ellis at one of his 'joints', a place that was more brothel than club. 'That must have been the place Ruth told me about,' Estelle said, 'the place where she worked before she started at the Sly Fox. An unhappy place for her.'

'I met her once,' Amelia Constant recalled, 'and I know that she had some terrible experiences, poor girl. We must try to save her from this horrible death sentence.'

'This is such an awful business,' Benny said afterwards, at Estelle's flat. 'Your poor friend. She's had a harsh time over the years.'

'I know,' Estelle said as she sank into a chair and closed her eyes. 'I feel guilty about boasting to her about how strong I felt when I brandished that gun in Jamaica. Some people call guns equalisers,' she continued after a short pause without opening her eyes. 'Did you know that?' she asked, somewhat blearily.

Benny ignored her question and instead put one to her: 'What happened to that gun? I've often wondered ever since you told me you'd brought it back on the cruise liner. Sam got hold of it for me. I still owe him for it. I keep meaning to ask you but never remember, until now.'

'I don't know,' she shot back, unexpectedly aggressively, her eyes now open wide. 'I somehow managed to lose it. Don't you think I feel bad enough recommending it to her – for revenge! – without you implying that I supplied the murder weapon? Not to mention the danger I put myself in for smuggling the bloody thing across the ocean. Twice.'

She closed her eyes and sighed before crying out: 'I lost it. All right? I'm sorry. I've searched for it but haven't found it. Some of those lizards who hung around with Monty kept asking to see it, or borrow or buy it. I did show it around and maybe lent it to one or two of the girls to show off. I lost interest in it.'

'Did you ask Ruth where she got her gun?' Benny resumed his interrogation. 'The one, whosoever it was, that ended her boyfriend's life.'

'I didn't know she had a gun before she used it. I did try to ask her when I saw her in Holloway. She tried to hint but you can't say much in prison. You're being watched and your conversation listened to all the time.' Estelle shifted uneasily in her chair.

'She didn't need to kill him,' Benny said. 'It didn't need to come to that.'

'How would you know?' Estelle screamed.

This was the one, solitary flash of anger that she directed at Benny throughout their long affair. And even that was smoothed over within an hour, with Estelle clinging to Benny as she sobbed into a shirt that Bertha had bought him for his thirty-sixth birthday.

But it was this moment that Benny would look back upon as the one in which he realised that that he didn't have what it takes for a man, secure in his surroundings, to overturn the pillars of his existence. To leave Bertha, his home and Excelsior Arcade and somehow spirit Estelle away into an unknown and unsheltered paradise. But such was his longing that he was compelled for many more years to act as if that were still possible.

'I suppose,' he mused in his journal, decades on, in the eventual time of his looking back, 'I wanted her to break it off rather than summon up the courage to do it myself, partly because I couldn't believe that she could possibly go on wanting to be with me as much as I wanted to be with her, partly because I didn't want to be the one who did the dastardly deed, and partly because, deep down, I didn't want to leave Bertha. As Estie often said to me, "You can't fix everything, Mister Fixer."'

Three

The boxer, Joseph Campbell, of London, whose victory by a knockout over Yorkshire's Dennis Martin on Wednesday put him in a leading position to challenge the European middleweight champion Tiberio Mitri, is feared missing. Close friends described him as having driven away in his sports car from Shoreditch Town Hall, where the bout took place, immediately after having washed and changed out of his boxing apparel. Scotland Yard has appealed for information regarding the disappearance, in the first instance by dialling Whitehall 1212.

Mr Campbell's landlady, Mrs Maud Gawler, told police that Mr Campbell – better known in pugilistic circles as Kid Joey – had arrived back home in an agitated state and then driven off to leave his car overnight outside the garage of M&A motors, half a mile from his home, so that they could repair a small fault early the next morning. The next evening, Mrs Gawler explained, she discovered that Mr Campbell had not returned and she telephoned the police. It appears that none of his friends knew of his present whereabouts. Mr Leslie Walker, the manager of M&A Motors said he knew of no arrangement with Mr Campbell to repair his car – which had not been left outside his garage.

'CHAMPIONSHIP CONTENDER GOES MISSING AFTER TRIUMPH',
THE TIMES, APRIL, 1954

In his journal, under the cutting of the *Times* news item about Joey the Boxer's disappearance in the wake of his victory over Butch Martin, Benny had written: 'This was one of the strangest of nights. Sam and I went to see Joey the Kid expecting that he would, in Sam's words, 'annihilate some flabby loser from up north', whom he had already beaten a few months earlier, which would put him in line for a crack at the British title and even the European, held by Tiberio Mitri, who beat Joey's idol, Randolph Turpin.

'But the Kid seemed to find it a struggle. He looked good, muscles and eyes gleaming, rhythmic shadow boxing, the usual ritual, but he didn't seem good mentally. He frowned his way through the fight and argued with his seconds between rounds. It looked like our expectations, and those of the rest of Joey's noisy supporters, were going to be dashed.

'And then, in the very last round, the Kid pulled himself out of the doldrums and turned into a high-speed punching machine. His poor opponent didn't know where he was, and the referee (Frank Musoe from Shoreditch) was very slow in rescuing him from further punishment. The poor sod could have died. It was sensational stuff. Miserable Monty Berman was among the spectators and even he was cheering. The noise of the crowd almost drowned Vera Coleman's high-pitched screams coming from a few rows behind us. Almost, but not quite.

'Little Jack was sitting opposite us on the other side of the ring and he rushed out of his seat at the fight's climax, probably, I said to Sam, to tell Joey where he'd gone wrong in the early rounds. What an arrogant *mumser*. Funny to think how we were really quite friendly in the army.

'Sam and I were in good spirits on the drive home and laughed at how Monty Berman managed to crawl out of his precious club and let his hair down for once. Such a comical sight.

'After I'd dropped Sam off, I drove back to the house happily whistling. But when I arrived at my front door, Bertha was waiting just behind it, looking angry and apprehensive. "You've got visitors," she said, her voice sharp. "They've been here about a quarter of an hour. Well, not here exactly. Across the road. In that red car parked over there. Two blokes: one – a tough-looking specimen – came over and knocked on the door asking for you, while the other one stayed in the car, slumped in the back seat. I couldn't see his face. He was covered up by his hat and coat. I said you weren't home yet but shouldn't be long. The tough guy said they'd wait in the car.'

'Having seen me,' Benny wrote, 'the same man crossed the road and introduced himself as Joey Campbell's assistant trainer. He had brought the Kid to see me urgently. "He's in my car now," he said quietly. "It's important you speak to him. Help him."'

In Benny's journal, there followed a rambling, breathless and sometimes cryptic account of a fighter whose head, less than a couple of hours earlier in a packed arena, had resounded with the massive roar of an ardent crowd, and whose eyes had been dazzled by the flashing of scores of cameras, now almost breaking down in Bertha and Benny's kitchen.

Inevitably, Little Jack Lewis was at the heart of it. Not, as Eddie Lawrence would later claim, because of a perceived relationship between Joey and Little Jack's wife Renée, but because, when it came to the bell at the start of the last round, Joey failed to stick to the lucrative arrangement he had been coerced into by Little Jack to throw the fight – an outcome in which Jack had a massive financial stake.

'I couldn't go through with it,' Joey told Benny, through his tears. 'I had the beating of Butch from the start. I could have had him in the fourth or fifth. As I got up for the last round, I saw evil Little Jack staring at me from his privileged seat. And as I turned my gaze into Butch's sweaty face it seemed to fade and change into the face of a different person altogether. I felt my whole body swelling, gathering strength, and then I launched that big attack. It wasn't poor old Butch I was aiming at. It was Little Jack.'

Once Benny had arranged with Maxie the Ganoff for Joey Campbell to hunker down for a few days, weeks or longer if necessary at Maxie's 'secret' cottage in Kent, and packed the Kid's assistant trainer off to drive him there, he sat down with Bertha at their kitchen table, heaped an extra spoonful of sugar into a mug of strong tea and said: 'This is a real mess, Berth.'

'I don't understand why Joey should be so scared of Little Jack,' Bertha said. 'He's a professional fighter. Why should he worry about that slimy creep?'

'That's a very naïve question,' said Benny.

Four

A verdict of misadventure was recorded at the South London Coroners' Court this week regarding the death of the successful and popular furniture dealer Jack Sidney Lewis. Mr Lewis, of Streatham, who died at the end of last month, was a well-known, colourful figure in Brixton, where he was the proprietor of Lewis and Son furniture store in Acre Lane, inside which, or outside in the summer, he could frequently be seen smoking a large cigar. Mr Lewis was also the major shareholder in the Jax jazz club in Richmond, which he founded and where he was found dead, reportedly having shot himself. No motive is known for this alleged act.

SOUTH LONDON PRESS, MARCH 1976

D avy and Netta Greenhouse had long been planning and looking forward to celebrating their daughter Melanie's engagement to Colin Levitt, a trainee lawyer from Leeds. And they decided to throw a party at the smart Turret Hotel in Hertfordshire, with a banquet, a string quartet and eighty guests.

On the day, when the party was almost over, Morrie Meadows, the nefariously connected caterer from Brixton who had supplied the food and drink, asked Davy if he could speak to him in private. This, it turned out, was to pass on the news – which Morrie had just received – that Little Jack Lewis was dead. Morrie had no idea of the cause of death, he said. He just knew the bare fact.

Davy spoke to Netta, Melanie and Colin and they agreed that Davy should make an announcement, which he did after the string quartet had put away their instruments. Once everyone who was still left in the Turret ballroom had responded to the call for silence, Davy's short, solemn statement drew a collective gasp. This was prompted not so much by the death itself as by Fancy Goods Harry's shocking reaction to it in front of the remaining party guests: 'Good riddance to that *mumser*. The world's a better place with him dead.'

But then, Fancy Goods Harry Miller had recently become much more open-mouthed and candid generally, his wife, Celia, having finally found out about his twenty-odd year relationship with Vera Coleman. He felt peculiarly liberated from the strain of keeping it secret for so long.

He and Vera, who owned the 'Upon My Sole' shoe shop in Brixton Road, had first met in the mid-1950s at the party celebrating Bertha and Benny Pomeranski's tenth wedding anniversary in their house in Brixton, where Estelle Davis sang a song of secret love, which was an appropriate choice in relation to herself and her host, Benny, and at the same time prescient in relation to Vera and Harry, whose affair was about to begin – just as Harry's fancy-goods business was taking off.

Vera had come to the party from King's College Hospital, where she'd been visiting her husband, who'd had his appendix removed. Meanwhile, Celia Miller, Harry's wife, was taking part in a dress rehearsal of *The Importance of Being Earnest* with her amateur dramatic group. It was also obligatory for cast members to attend the post-rehearsal party, and the combination of the two events would keep her away much longer than the Pomeranski anniversary celebrations would last.

At that anniversary party, when Benny urged his guests to form themselves into couples to dance to a selection of records he had chosen, and Estelle acted as dance hostess encouraging everyone to lose his or her inhibitions, the showy extrovert Vera and the normally quiet joker Harry were thrown together and (as 'Fancy Goods' quaintly put it to 'the Fixer') they almost immediately 'clicked'. Harry gave Vera a lift home from the party and what followed was, in the strange, elated phrase of a pleased-with-himself Harry when confiding his secret to Benny, *'click clock'*.

But when, at a different party, years later, the now far-from-quiet Harry Miller caused a great stir with his public curse directed at the recently deceased Little Jack, he reined in any traces of facetious humour, limiting himself to a happy grin at Little Jack's departure.

When the official suicide verdict was released, creating a widespread sense of shock, nobody pointed the finger at Sam the Stick – at least, not openly. And the police were uninterested in taking their investigations further. It all seemed cut and dried. Even Renée, Jack Lewis's wife, was privately satisfied enough to cash in the insurance policy.

But, while it was never said aloud that Sam might have helped Little Jack on his way, there were plenty of whispers. Two local businessmen, who for years had been under Little Jack's 'protection', stopped Sam in the street to shake his hand, one of them thanking him quite emotionally. Sam affected not to know what the man was talking about, which produced a wink from the other businessman.

However, not all the whispered speculation surrounding Jack Lewis's spectacular end was couched in gratitude to Sam. Although Renée Lewis accepted the coroner's verdict (and the insurance pay out) and was supported in her loss by her daughter Bonnie (whose mourning for Little Jack was far deeper than her mother's), Renée's son, Ronnie, who had always admired his father's way of achieving and exercising power and aspired to emulate him, was certain Little Jack had been murdered.

Now was the time, Ronnie Lewis reasoned, to make good his ambition of following in his father's footsteps. For he was convinced that Little Jack would never have even contemplated suicide – and Ronnie had Samuel Golub in his sights.

When, at the Jax's muted reopening after the boss's death, Little Jack's clarinet-playing employee Eddie Lawrence asked Benny, in a confidential undertone, if 'any of your boys had anything to do with Little Jack's strangely abrupt ending', the Fixer assured him he was as surprised as anyone else. Eddie described his boss's death as 'the most unexpected thing I can remember in my whole life. And the only one of your boys with the motive – so I've heard – or the nerve – to slaughter Little Jack is Sam the Stick. Ronnie refuses to believe his dad topped himself and reckons Sam could well have done it.

'But,' Eddie added, using his hands to make a contradictory gesture, 'as it happens, Sammy was actually downstairs with me here at the jazz club round about the time of Jack's death, busy cutting Big Bill Crowe down to size.

'My wife Karina tells me that most suicides come out of the blue,' Eddie continued. 'And that when men kill themselves there's always a woman involved. Karina's heard that Jack was havin' it off with Joyce, Sam's missis. And that Jack's own missis, the lovely Renée, has been havin' it off with Joey Campbell. They reckon that's why Joey did a runner after his fight with Butch Martin. Little Jack had found out and was furious.'

'Tongues will always wag,' Benny said, wearily shaking his head.

'That's as maybe,' Eddie said with a shrug, 'but now Ronnie needs a culprit. And, it seems, the pair he refers to as the Cripple and the Slugger, wherever he may be, fit the bill.'

'Eddie,' said Benny, placing a hand on Eddie's shoulder and lowering his voice a little more, 'I think you should be very careful not to spread incriminating gossip about Kid Joey. And I especially strongly advise you not to call Sammy Golub a "cripple".'

'Oh, please, Benny, I do know better than that. I was just communicating Little Ronnie's words.'

'I know you were, Eddie my man, but try not to spread them around. And, by the way, I'm hoping to hear you play your liquorice stick tonight.'

'You will, Benny. The family have asked me to play "Summertime", Little Jack's favourite song they tell me. Who knew?'

'That will be a genuine treat, Eddie... Hey, just a minute, isn't that Frank Musoe, the boxing referee, over there going to Renée's table?'

'I believe it is. I know he and LJ used to have the odd drink together. Jack used to advise him about making decisions in the ring, I believe, if you know what I mean,' said Eddie with a wink. At which, the two men parted in laughter.

Benny's first reaction upon hearing the news of Little Jack's passing had been to phone his oldest comrade. 'Sam, we need to speak,' he said. 'At your place when Joyce is out at work.' (Joyce's latest employment was as a nine-to-five clerical worker for the local council at Lambeth Town Hall, no more than fifty yards from Little Jack's furniture office and showroom, of which Ronnie Lewis, immediately after his father's funeral, announced himself as sole proprietor.)

'Why not the Astoria café?' Sam asked with alarming composure.

'Because we need to be private, you daft *lobbes*,' Benny replied, using the term for 'rascal' that Jewish parents in those days used, mostly endearingly, when chiding their sons for cheeky misbehaviour. But Little Jack had frequently used the word condescendingly when addressing Sam over the years, to the latter's deep irritation. 'Ah, here comes the *lobbes* hobbling along,' Jack would say. 'How're you doing, little *lobbes*?'

The most notorious instance was when Jack stood up amid scores of guests at an event at Streatham's Orthodox synagogue and accompanied his supercilious words with elaborate arm gestures: 'Look, is this Moses with his staff ready to strike the rock? Oh, no, it's only a little *lobbes* with a stick. What a disappointment!'

Benny came straight to the point once he and Sam were seated in Sam and Joyce's living room facing each other across a table upon which Sam had placed two glasses of Scotch. 'How on earth did you manage it?' Benny asked animatedly.

'Manage what?'

'Your philanthropic masterpiece by the river at Richmond,' said Benny as he smiled his approval.

'Phil *who*?'

'You know what I'm bloody well talking about, you dark little horse.'

'Well, maybe I would if you didn't use such *shprauncy* language,' Sam responded with an enormous smile. At which, Benny stood, took hold of his glass of whisky, held it up high and, after shaking his head from side to side a couple of times and smiling, declared: 'Here's to absent bastards!'

'To absent bastards,' echoed Sam 'the Stick' Golub, the triumphant *kalikah*, as he mimed an exaggerated spitting action at the floor before sinking his whisky. 'To absent bastards!'

'Or better,' Benny amended his words for a second toast: 'To the absence of bastards.'

Five

As the cortège left Kingston, it passed by the house at 56 Hope Road whose walls still bore the scars from the bullets that narrowly failed to kill Marley in a politically motivated attack in 1976. On South Camp Road, outside the Alpha Boys School, where many of Jamaica's finest musicians had been taught to play by an inspiring teacher named Ruben Delgado, pupils sang 'No Woman, No Cry' as the procession headed towards Marcus Garvey Drive and out of the city on the road towards Spanish Town.

THE GUARDIAN, MAY 1981

In mid-May 1981, underneath a cutting from a feature in the *Guardian* newspaper describing the atmosphere at the recent funeral of the Jamaican singer Bob Marley, Benny Pomeranski wrote in his personal journal: 'JC has sent me a photograph of himself with Bob Marley taken three years ago. It is tucked in among the photographs alongside this journal in the big folder.

'I was never especially interested in calypso, reggae, or any other Jamaican music,' Benny blandly went on, 'despite (or perhaps because of) hearing it all day long, pouring, and sometimes booming, out of Harvey Constant's record shop a few doors along from us in Excelsior Arcade. And I hadn't ever knowingly heard Bob Marley sing, but JC seemed to revere him and was devastated when he died.

'He enclosed a letter with the photo, telling me how significant Marley was in contemporary Jamaican life and how sad he was because Marley's death had not only driven what seemed to be the whole island into a state of mourning, but it had come at a time when things in general weren't exactly glowing for JC himself. As I knew only too well. He and I had had virtually no business contact for months, after many productive years. He hinted about retiring.'

A few years later, Benny looked back at these events in his journal narrative – 'I was worried about him at the time,' he wrote, 'but he seemed to get himself back together quite quickly' – going on to recall how he had been much more concerned a few years later when many Caribbean businesses were ruined by the tropical cyclone 'Hurricane Gilbert' hitting Kingston.

'Homes were wrecked and about fifty people lost their lives in Jamaica while the hurricane claimed over four hundred throughout the Caribbean region,' Benny wrote. 'Massive flooding caused still more damage. There was looting, food riots and general chaos. More than £50 million-worth of goods were purloined. Even the emergency shelters were destroyed. Jamaica's banana industry was annihilated to the tune of £400 million. Some 7,500 acres of the banana crop were destroyed. JC couldn't leave his home, which luckily still stood after the hurricane, though some windows were shattered.

'And,' Benny reported, 'in the middle of it all, JC managed to get a call through to me to reassure me that he was safe and that he still loved Jamaica.'

At this point in his journal, Benny took up two whole pages to heap praise upon Lionel Solomons. He began by writing about Lionel's dramatic escape from Poland before the Nazis invaded. In this, Lionel and a handful of other members of his family were assisted by a British-born distant cousin, Max Goodman, who also happened to be Benny Pomeranski's own cousin and who had gone to live in Miami in America in the 1920s. All but one of those members of the Solomons family who stayed behind in Poland perished in the concentration camps.

Benny said Lionel was possessed of 'the life force' and how he admired him for his deep love of his wife Irene and their children, and for his kindness, 'especially to JC'. He extolled Lionel's 'amazing resourcefulness. He was the supreme fixer,' Brixton's own fixer wrote, and gave three examples of Lionel's fixing skills. As Simon Pomeranski read these, he reacted to each one with a perplexed laugh and an increasingly astonished exclamation.

Firstly, Benny recited, stage by stage, Lionel's generosity to Jeff Calloway, especially in he and his wife Irene welcoming the young immigrant into their home. He then stated his admiration for Lionel's knowing exactly how to disburse (and cash in on) the Farringdon diamonds, and his calm and efficient way of doing so.

Finally, Benny revealed how Lionel had already paved the way for JC's smooth assimilation into life in Kingston by 'magically' securing false documents, including a passport, that transformed British boxer Joseph Campbell into Jamaican textile trader Jeffrey Calloway – named after Lionel Solomons's favourite jazz musician, Cab Calloway.

Six

Not only did Ronnie Lewis inherit a flourishing furniture business and an impressive amount of cash from his father, but around half-a-dozen of Little Jack's hired hands and henchmen said they were happy to stay loyal to his chip-off-the-block son.

Ronnie detected, or thought he did, a certain condescending reluctance among a couple of the older and rougher individuals and tended to rely on the two or three he felt he could trust. Accordingly, he reduced the manifestly trustworthy Eddie Lawrence's duties at the jazz club – which Ronnie kept open with a scaled-down programme – and leaned on him for general and confidential help and advice in matters legal and illegal.

Eddie was not entirely comfortable with this arrangement – especially as Ronnie remained obsessed with avenging Little Jack's death – but he was handsomely paid. Moreover, he was freer to play his clarinet at Jax than he had been in Little Jack's day. He also, to his own surprise as much as that of others, displayed a confident ability to run and reinvigorate the Lewis and Son company's furniture business.

The extent of Ronnie Lewis's obsession with his father's death was such that it led him to reveal the names of his personal prime suspects to the police – in the shape of Sergeant Reg Surple, with whom Little Jack had himself managed to remain on amicable terms over the years.

'Much as the lads at Brixton Station would love to put Sam the Stick away,' Reg Surple responded to Ronnie's accusations, 'unfortunately he has an alibi. Witnesses say that he was downstairs at the bar in the jazz club at the very moment your father died upstairs in his office. Sorry, Ronnie.'

'But that's just it,' Ronnie persisted. 'He was in the club premises at the relevant moment. Nobody knows the precise second that it happened. He could have sneaked upstairs away from the crowd and back without being noticed. Or he could have come into the club and killed my dad before he actually went to the bar.'

'That's extremely unlikely,' said Surple. 'There's absolutely no evidence for it and, anyway, forensics say it all points to suicide. A classic case.'

'Sam Golub is a violent man,' Ronnie Lewis replied. 'He assaulted Bill Crowe, an old friend of my father's, on that very day in the club. And Golub had motives for killing Little Jack. For one, he must have really resented that there was somebody in Brixton who was so much scarier than he was. Somebody who commanded a hundred times more respect. But, more than that, people were accusing my dad – behind his back of course – of having it off with Sam Golub's wife, Joyce. And what was Golub doing at Jax anyway? He very rarely went there and when he did it was always with his minder, Pomeranski. But on that occasion he was alone.'

'I know about Big Bill's encounter with the charming Sam the Stick,' said Reg Surple. 'I've spoken to Bill myself, who is clearly embarrassed by the whole business. He emphatically did not wish to press charges. "Leave it to me" is what he said. I did my duty and warned him off any rough stuff. "Rough stuff, me? Of course not," he said. Ha, ha, I thought. Very funny. Big Bill is not a man to let something like that lie. But he needs to be careful.

'As for Sam Golub's presence in the jazz club, Eddie Lawrence will tell you, as he told me, that Golub was there to talk to your father about a possible loan to help Golub's old mum, who was having problems paying her rent and making ends meet.'

'You said you had two suspects,' Surple continued. 'So who's the other joker? Are you claiming that whoever it is did the deed together with Sam Golub?'

'No, but, well, this is a bit upsetting because my dad was extremely helpful to him and I used to hero-worship him. It's Joey Campbell.'

'The boxer who did a runner? Kid Joey?'

'That's right, the cocky bastard who lived in our house when he was young, thanks to my dad's kindness, and your lot still haven't found him. And again, my suspicion is based on what lots of people say. If so many say it, it is quite probably true, isn't it? Smoke without fire and all that. Worth investigating.'

'So what are people saying?'

'That Joey tried it on with my mum.' Ronnie took a deep breath before continuing: 'This is hard to deal with. He lived in our house for a couple of years when I was a kid. I honestly looked up to him. Some reckon that Kid Joey was trying to persuade my mum to leave my dad and run away with him.'

'Really? She was quite a bit older than he was.'

'I know, but I was there when my dad more or less accused him – in front of several others.'

'We haven't solved the Kid's vanishing act, in spite of colleagues of mine spending a great deal of time and money trying to find out what's happened to him,' Surple firmly asserted. 'He may be no longer alive for all that is known. So, I'm afraid your Joseph Campbell is currently beyond questioning about his reasons for absconding – if that's what he did.'

'So, that's two cases your people have completely failed on. You can't find a famous sportsman with a still-quite-famous face who's hiding – he's not dead, believe me – and you can't nail the person who has killed a prominent South London businessman, and they might be one and the same.'

'There's no solving required in the second case now,' Reg said in a sombre tone. 'I'm truly sorry, Ronnie, it must be very hard for you, but you're going to have to accept that your father took his own life.'

'No I don't have to accept that,' said Ronnie, fighting off tears. 'I won't. I'll never accept that my father committed suicide. Why would he?'

Not only was Joey the Boxer untraceable, but the Astorian protective armour around Sam the Stick was far too strong for Ronnie Lewis to penetrate. And, although he was inclined to believe that Sam Golub was his father's killer, he also could not shake off the possibility that Joey Campbell, too, wanted Little Jack out of the way.

He remembered that Renée, his mother, always spoke well of Joey and that Joey was clearly very fond of her, devoted even. He had once intervened in a bitter shouting match between Ronnie's parents, daring to tell Jack that he should apologise to Renée. Later that day, with Little Jack out of the house, Ronnie was walking quietly along the hall when he witnessed through the open kitchen door his mother put her arms around Joey and say, 'Thank you, you're a darling.' And Joey did not exactly resist. 'He was obviously flattered,' Ronnie later told his sister Bonnie. Both of them, he told Reg Surple, were too shocked at the time to make anything more of it.

However split Ronnie's suspicions were, he needed to 'put right' the situation, to repay the destruction of his previously indestructible father. And since he couldn't decide one hundred per cent that Sam had been responsible, because of his nagging concern that Joey might have been, he decided he would just have to kill them both.

Seven

It was towards the end of the year of 1981 that Sam the Stick decided to paint his kitchen. It had irked him for years that the paintwork was not only in a poor state, but also afforded both him and Joyce – especially him – a constant and seemingly permanent reminder of Joyce's former Italian lover (the Neapolitan bell-chime she had brought from her flat had long been dispensed with).

Roberto had originally painted the entire kitchen white and Sam decided upon a dark shade of olive green to obliterate it. He was making good, gratifying progress when, reaching for a difficult spot in a corner just beneath the picture rail, the ladder he was standing on tilted and swayed under his weight and he crashed to the marble-tiled floor.

His 'good' leg took the brunt of it and he called out in agony. Joyce wasted no time and phoned for an ambulance. She went with him to the hospital and alternately stood or sat watching him being processed through initial examination to temporary bandaging and a place in a bed in the Annie Zunz ward. She was given a lift home by a tweedy, silver-haired lady member of the 'hospital friends' so that she could gather together pyjamas, underwear and various other necessities for Sam while Maud, the hospital friend, sat sipping a cup of tea in Joyce and Sam's 'best' room.

'I won't be long,' Joyce called out from the kitchen where she was searching for a recently bought packet of Sam's favourite chocolate biscuits.

'Oh, take your time, my dear,' Maud replied in a euphonious home-counties accent. 'There's no rush. I am enjoying my cup of tea on your lovely, comfortable sofa. I must say, you do keep your home spick and span.'

By the time they got back to the hospital ward, Sam was asleep. The nurse taking care of him advised Joyce to let him sleep for a little longer and have a cup of tea herself in the canteen.

'I've put some of his favourite biscuits in his bedside-table cupboard,' Joyce informed the nurse. 'Will they be all right there?'

'Oh, that's nice,' said the nurse. 'Yes, they'll be fine there. Come back in about a quarter of an hour when the doctor is due. We'll wake your husband then and you and he can ask the doctor any questions you might have.'

Sam's injuries turned out to be more complicated than expected and later that evening he was transferred to a different ward. Again, Joyce accompanied him. 'Don't forget your chocolate biscuits,' she reminded him. 'Don't forget my stick,' he urged her.

He was kept in hospital for several weeks and when he eventually came home to find that Joyce had turned the sofa into a bed, he found it hard to sleep on. On his second day home, he had a fall and was promptly readmitted to the hospital. Joyce told the staff that she couldn't manage and they helped her to find him a place in a care home in Streatham.

At first, Sam rebelled against the move but once he had spent a couple of days at Valley Ridge Nursing Home, run by the local council, he found it far more comfortable – and less intrusively medical – than the hospital, and indeed than home.

Joyce came to see him most days and he even made a friend. Berlin-born George Cowan, an elderly fellow-resident, twenty years Sam's senior, was a survivor of Dachau extermination camp and had been in the nursing home for almost a year. In conversation with George, Sam for the first time in his life found himself speaking about his mother's aunt and other relatives who had been murdered by the Nazis.

His mother had never really overcome the shock of hearing, on the eve of Sam's wedding to Joyce, the news that her aunt Eva and two cousins had perished in Treblinka. As far as Sam could remember, ever since he and Joyce had set up home in a flat very near to the house in which he had grown up, nobody had uttered a word about this appalling discovery, or its timing.

Sam himself could recall his great-aunt Eva having come from Poland to attend his bar mitzvah, a poignant event since he had to read his portion of the law supported by a wooden crutch on one side and his father on the other. And even more poignant in retrospect because, all the time Eva was in Britain for the bar mitzvah, she steadfastly resisted the concerted pleas by family and friends, at both the service and the party that followed, to leave Warsaw and find a place to live in London.

That same year, Adolf Hitler was elected to power in Germany. Six years later, the Germans invaded Poland, followed by the Soviets, and Eva's husband took his own life. Eva and their two adult children were placed in the Warsaw Ghetto, from where, in 1942, they were taken to Treblinka extermination camp. Their deaths were not officially ratified until after the war, in 1946.

George Cowan was an intelligent and loquacious individual, able to draw Sam into quite long conversations – admittedly in which George did most of the talking – and, although their initial exchanges were largely about George's capture, incarceration and torture, these were far from being mournful and they soon extended into other subjects.

Sam found George both interesting and amusing and came to relish his company. George, too, welcomed Sam's attention and the two of them spent hours discussing a range of topics from films to football. At times, Sam was on the brink of confessing to George his slaying of Little Jack and other dark deeds, but he always managed to hold back. He did wonder, however, whether he would have been able to do so had he not had Benny Pomeranski as his oldest and still-present friend.

Eight

It didn't take long for Ronnie Lewis to find out that Sam – 'no doubt with his stick' – was resident at Valley Ridge Nursing Home in Streatham. And, within hours of this tantalising discovery, he was fervently plotting, his obsessive temperament having completely taken him over. Eddie Lawrence was now a virtual one-man confidant to whom fell the management of Ronnie's obsession, which Eddie longed to bring to an end. But Ronnie wouldn't let it go.

'Eddie,' he asked one morning, 'what do you think about poison?'

'For Sam the Stick?'

'Yes, of course. For Sam the Stick. If you can think of a way to put some poison on his menu, without it being traced to where it came from, you're on to a big cash bonus on top of your pay. If we can get some poisoned food into him while he is being fed institutional grub in Valley Ridge – boiled fish, mashed potatoes, that sort of thing – we're on to a winner. What do you reckon, Eddie?'

'Shouldn't be a problem.'

'Do you know how to get an effective poison into food, without being rumbled?'

'I know of a way to put it into food,' he assured Ronnie, 'which makes it undetectable.'

'How do you know? Have you tried it?'

'Indirectly, yes.'

'What does that mean?'

'I helped to prepare a cake for someone in which he was going to insert a dodgy extra ingredient and then serve it up to the appropriate party. It was a payback. A nasty piece of work who had it coming. And I assumed it must have worked because the person who paid me to do it never asked for his money back.'

'And who was this dangerous cook? Anyone I know?'

'Oh, no, no, no. It was a long time ago.'

'How long ago?'

'Oh, a very long time. In Jamaica. And I was sworn to eternal secrecy, not ever to tell anyone, even you, Ronnie.'

'How about doing a bit of baking for me, then? As I said, you'll get paid handsomely and, if it works, I'll add in an extra bonus, on top of the first one. This means a lot to me.'

'Okay. What do you require?'

'A cake, I think. A fruit cake.'

'I can do that.'

'Wrapped up nicely and posted to a Mr S. Golub, care of Valley Ridge Nursing Home, London, SW16,' Ronnie told Eddie. 'Put a cherry on top. Enclose a card and, in fake handwriting, maybe using your wrong hand, put on it: "Dear Sam. Get well soon. Dave". That's the Golub brother who went to South Africa after the war and no one knows, or cares, what happened to him. It's thought he came back to London in about 1960. Sam hasn't spoken to him for about thirty years.'

'Clever.'

'You'll be on your own for this one,' said Ronnie, pushing the air with both open palms to indicate distance. 'I don't want anyone to be able put this on to me. So keep me out of the whole operation from start to finish. I don't want to have any visible connection. Don't tell me what the poison is, or where you get it from. It's best I don't know. But when the deed is done, come to me for your handsome handout of *gelt*. But remember, Eddie, there must be no trail leading back to us. That's me and *you*. So don't post the cake anywhere near here. And buy the essential ingredients in a big chemist's shop or whatever far away from here. Maybe two shops in two different places. And both very far from Brixton Road.'

'Don't worry, Ronnie. I'll take all necessary precautions.'

'Good. It won't give the cake a noticeable, weird taste will it?'

'No. It's completely absorbed. You'd never know there was something untoward. It'll be exactly as if nothing was added at all to the original ingredients.'

'Brilliant, Eddie. You know, I think you were wasted spending so much of your time at the jazz club. My dad clearly didn't recognise your full qualities. Unusual for him.'

Eddie's reaction to that comment remained inside his head, an unspoken thought: 'Unlike you, your dad knew what he was doing and he knew I was not at ease with killing and violence. It was my clarinet he employed me for, and he paid well. His love of jazz was one of the few good things about Little Jack. "You make a sound like a beautiful bird," he used to say to me. And, as nasty as he was, he would not have been so stupid as to ask me about poison.'

Two days later, Ronnie Lewis took Eddie Lawrence out for a 'special thank you' lunch. They met in a restaurant in Clapham. Ronnie was feverishly impatient and, as soon as he arrived at the table that he'd booked, and at which Eddie was already sitting reading an old copy of *Jazz Journal*, asked, before sitting down, 'Where did you post it from?'

'In the West End,' Eddie said. 'Near Trafalgar Square.'

'Excellent. Will it have arrived at Valley Ridge by now?'

'I would have thought so.'

'How long does it take to work?'

'I reckon it'll be less than a few hours. It'll probably be night-time and they'll think it's just one of the old inmates having a bit of a stomach ache. People at institutions like Valley Ridge die all the time. Routine stuff.'

While Ronnie Lewis was ordering a bottle of Pinot Noir in Clapham, a nurse in Valley Ridge left a package – on the outside reading 'From Brother Dave' – on Sam the Stick's bedside cabinet.

Sam was, as had become customary, in the residents' lounge with George. When he returned, rather earlier than normal owing to George's feeling a little unwell, he was both intrigued and sceptical as he tried unsuccessfully to open the package, which Eddie had firmly sealed in with packaging tape. 'Gosh, that's a tough one, Sam,' said a passing nurse, seeing him struggling. 'Here, give it to me. I've got some scissors. Let me open it.'

To say Sam Golub was surprised to receive a package from his long-lost brother would be a twenty-carat understatement. 'That bastard probably thought I'm at death's door,' he told the nurse. 'And that probably cheered up the old sod no end. I wonder who told him I was here. They can only have bumped into him by accident. I haven't a clue where he's living.

'D'you know, we each promised to spit, or dance, on the grave of the other, whichever one of us dies first. He's probably getting his old dancing shoes on as we speak. Well, that's tough, old brother. It's not gonna be me. I am going to outlive you.

'What exactly is it?' Sam asked as the nurse pulled away the wrapping.

'It's a fruit cake,' she said. 'A small one. Looks nice. And there's a card wishing you better. From Dave.'

'I don't like cake,' Sam said. 'Especially fruit cake. And even more especially a fruit cake that comes from a nasty bastard of a brother, even if he is doing a good deed for once in his selfish, arrogant life. Tell you what, darlin' – give it to George. He hasn't been well and he'll love it. He's always eating sweet things.'

'All right, Sam. Pity to waste it,' said the nurse, with a motherly smile. 'You're right, George will love it.'

Eddie Lawrence was right about the 'routine stuff'. A night-nurse was called that night to investigate one of the residents, namely George Cowan, complaining of pains, and gave him something to help him to sleep. All that did was quieten the poor man's groans. He died an hour or so before dawn.

Nine

When Benny heard of Sam's decorating accident, he was concerned but at the same time confidently expected his old childhood partner-in-mischief to climb back as he always had done. The original damage done to the young Samuel among the tramlines of Commercial Road in 1932 would always remain the touchstone.

Moreover, Benny's heavily pregnant daughter-in-law Marina went into labour the day after Sam's accident and gave birth that night in King's College Hospital, less than a stone's throw from Dulwich Hospital where Sam had been taken. The next day, Benny went from one hospital to the other, joyous at the arrival of his long-awaited first grandchild, William – always to be known as 'Will' – and, at that stage, not too disturbed by his oldest and most resilient friend's decorating calamity.

The birth of Will Pomeranski brought a smile, too, to the face of Sam Golub, on Benny's first visit to him in Dulwich Hospital, for a while lifting him out of his constant pain and discomfort. '*Mazeltov*, my old friend. I know you've been waiting a long time for this,' he said as he embraced an emotional Benjamin Pomeranski, grandfather, before going on to explain how he had come to be up that ladder and then fallen from it.

'I was trying to get at that Italian *mumser* by painting over his handiwork,' Sam told Benny. 'Clearing out all traces of him in my home.' Bertha was arriving later with Joyce, and Sam didn't want the women to know of his private motivation and the biting eagerness with which he had approached the task – and which no doubt was what landed him on his back in a hospital bed.

'Well, I hope this has got that old anger out of your system,' was Benny's reaction. 'Why am I always having to tell you to take it easy? Why don't you listen to me? I'm sure Joyce has long since forgotten the mini-Michelangelo. You are incorrigible.'

'Oh, here he is again with his fancy words. Incorrigibobbel,' a smiling Sam the Stick said loudly enough for the rest of the ward to hear. And, on subsequent visits, with or without Bertha, Benny was able, as always, to soothe Sam's bitterness with laughter – and a few photographs of the newest member of the Pomeranski clan.

But when his old running mate was admitted to Valley Ridge, Benny was much more distressed. He visited Sam regularly and always came away saddened. 'I don't think he's ever going to come out of there,' he told Bertha after only a couple of visits, and never saw fit to change that view.

The one bright spot was that Sam had befriended George Cowan who, on Benny's visits to Sam, spoke to both men and calmly answered their questions about his horrifying experiences. But he also spoke about his career as an optician in central London and how he had joined a volunteering group whose members were all survivors of the death camps and who gave a lot of their time to talk in schools with a view to instilling in the children the need to recognise evil and act to defeat it.

Most of the time, however, George chatted cheerfully and told jokes. And when Benny and Sam told him that he was brave, he brushed it aside: 'In what way am I brave? I had no choice. What I was, was lucky.' And he then went on to tell them both a joke.

He was still laughing and joking while gratefully devouring Sam's present of a fruit cake.

Large parts of Benny's journal were devoted to his thoughts about 'the Stick' during Sam's continuing residence in the care home. His condition did improve: he was allowed out of his bed to sit outside on one of the several benches around Valley Ridge, and even to walk a little along the grass-banked drive at the side of the building unaided other than by his stick – a new one supplied by the care home. But he tired rapidly and was exhausted by six o'clock most evenings. It became obvious that he would need round-the-clock care of the kind Joyce could not be expected to provide.

Following a post mortem, the announcement of George Cowan's death was delayed for a day or so before being attributed to 'natural causes' brought on by the pneumonia from which he was known to have been suffering. But Sam, who was badly affected by the loss of his recently acquired friend, did wonder if it could have been caused by the cake his brother Dave had sent, and whether the fraternal hostility had been strong enough for Dave to attempt to poison him.

Sam mentioned this to Benny, who, in order to support Sam, had hardly been away from the nursing home since George's death. About which, Sam told Benny, 'I'm feeling a bit guilty, which is very rare for me as you know.'

'It is a bit of a coincidence, I suppose, George passing away soon after noshing Dave's home-made cake,' Benny agreed. 'Let me do a bit of digging.'

It didn't take much digging for Benny to find out that Sam's brother David had, remarkably, died in Johannesburg only a few days before the unfortunate George Cowan in Streatham. 'So,' Benny reported to Sam, 'if Dave did send you that cake, it was one of his last acts on earth. And whether or not he did send it, you've got what you wanted – you outlived him.'

A nurse was standing at the end of Sam's bed when Benny broke the news of David Golub's death and Sam beckoned to her. 'I'm really upset about what happened to old George,' he said with uncharacteristic but palpable sympathy. 'I hope it was nothing to do with my cake.'

'No, of course it wasn't,' said the nurse with effusive reassurance.

'I know that people always say it's "natural causes",' Sam persisted, 'but that's just a generalisation. What did he actually die of? What killed him?'

'He had pneumonia,' the nurse said in a matter-of-fact tone, and then: 'See you in the morning, Sam. I'm about to finish my shift,' with a brisk smile that seemed to convey a let's-put-all-that-behind-us-and-carry-on sentiment.

Around the same time as this conversation was taking place in Valley Ridge, the telephone rang in Eddie Lawrence's office at Jax. When he picked it up, Eddie could hear Ronnie's voice, trembling and high-pitched, before he had even placed the receiver to his ear.

'Ronnie. Are you all right?'

'It didn't work.' Ronnie lowered his voice as he tried to compose himself.

'What didn't work?'

'What is the matter with you, Eddie? The fucking poison didn't work. I've been trying to find out for almost two days. It went wrong. It didn't work.'

'That's a shame.' Eddie was completely unflustered, nonchalant. He sounded almost indifferent. 'Maybe Sam's too much of a tough old—'

'No.' Ronnie, far from unflustered, interrupted him. 'No, it *did* work. But not on bloody Sam Golub. Some other poor old geezer copped it.'

'Erm.' Eddie was now the uneasy disbeliever. 'But... I don't understand.'

'What's to understand? The cake was sent to Sam. He passed it on to somebody else. It turns out Sam doesn't like cake. He hates it. So some other poor sod paid for Sam's fussy eating habits.'

'But what...' Eddie still seemed puzzled.

'What *is* the matter with you, Eddie? It's not your fault. You did your job. I can't believe my bad luck.'

'Yeah, it should have worked,' Eddie spoke hesitatingly, still sounding surprised, unable to take in what he'd been told and trying to pick his words carefully. He had prepared himself for an outcome at variance with the great revenge plan but an altogether different one from this new reality.

'Right, yes,' said Ronnie Lewis, who was becoming increasingly impatient. '*Yes* it should. It *should* have been eaten by the person it was addressed to. Sam Golub *should* have liked cake. Who the hell doesn't eat cake? *Everyone* likes cake. Don't worry, Eddie. You did your best. You'll still be paid. See you in the morning.'

Eddie Lawrence, both relieved and perplexed, put down the receiver, drew a deep breath, poured himself a beer – and began to laugh uncontrollably.

Ten

From Christmas in 1981 into the new year of 1982, Ronnie Lewis spent a month with his girlfriend Hazel in the house Little Jack had left to him in Altea on Spain's Costa Blanca. They hoped one day to make it their permanent home and both of them had started taking Spanish lessons. Ronnie always loved being there. It was the only place where he was able to relax and, on this occasion, he quickly felt more contented than he had been at any time in the five years since his father's death.

He had good reason to, though it took him a few moments to appreciate it. Within an hour of their arrival on the first day, Hazel – at twenty-eight, twelve years younger than Ronnie – had cooked and served up scrambled eggs with beans from a tin, poured them both a glass of Rioja, lifted her glass and announced, 'I've got some news, Ron. Can you guess what it is?'

At that point – his mind weighed down with matters back home, specifically how unjust life was and with the failure, in such unlikely and unlucky fashion, to pay back Sam the Stick – he swallowed the forkful of egg he was holding, looked almost distractedly at Hazel and said: 'No, what is it?'

Hazel's mouth briefly went from a downturn of disappointment into an indulgent smile. 'I'm pregnant,' she said.

'*What?*' Ronnie snapped out of his bleak reverie. 'Oh, God, I'm sorry! That's wonderful.'

At the end of their month's stay, having spoken to Eddie to catch up with routine business developments – all pursued in line with Ronnie's instruction for Eddie to 'keep it clean' while he was in Spain – and been assured that everything was 'sweetly ticking over', Ronnie phoned the agency through which his father had bought the house in Altea and enquired if there were any similar but slightly larger properties for sale in the local region.

'There definitely are but you need to speak to our owner, who deals personally with that area. He's abroad himself at the moment,' an earnest female cockney voice told him. 'Can it wait until next week? I can make an appointment with him for you. Are you thinking of selling your current property?'

'Well, yes, if there is something else available that suits us a little better.'

'Us?'

'Yes, my fiancée and myself.'

'Oh, lovely. Well, as you know, it's a great place for a young couple. I'll put you in the diary. How about Tuesday at four o'clock in the afternoon?'

'Yes, sure. I can do that. And what is your boss's name?'

'Mr William Crowe.'

'Ah, of course, yes.'

Ronnie at that moment recalled that 'Big Bill' Crowe had had something to do with Little Jack's purchase of the house in Spain and had little doubt that blind eyes had been turned and 'on the side' cash payments made in the course of the negotiations. He also remembered meeting Big Bill in person a couple of times at the Acre Lane showroom and once when he brought a party to the jazz club – though not on the day his father died and Bill Crowe was unlucky enough to run into Sam the Stick.

The following Tuesday, 'Mister William Crowe' was genial and expansive when Ronnie came to his Streatham High Road office, in the corner of which was a fridge, from where Bill brought out an expensive bottle of Chablis.

'This is a special occasion,' he said to his visitor, as he opened the bottle and took two glasses from a shelf. 'I can't tell you how pleased I am to see you. Your father and I went back a long way. I was devastated when he died. I was in the jazz club that very day but missed whatever happened on account of some creepy little gangster sneaking up on me from behind and injuring me with whatever blunt instrument he had with him. I had to get patched up at the hospital and they wouldn't let me go back to sort out the little runt.'

'That was Sam the Stick. Samuel Golub.'

'So I believe.'

'And you weren't the first and probably not the last to feel the weight of his no doubt reinforced walking stick. Did you know he's in a nursing home not ten minutes from this office?'

'*What?*' Bill Crowe removed from his mouth the just-lit cigarette he had placed there and aborted his inhalation with a spluttering cough.

'Yes. Valley Ridge,' Ronnie said before swallowing a generous mouthful of Chablis.

'My God, I know exactly where that is. Tell me, are you a friend of this Sam bastard?'

'Quite the opposite. I hate his guts. Always have done. It's good that he has ended up an old, helpless cripple rotting away in a care home. I believe he might have been responsible for my father's death.'

'Jack's death? But surely he—'

'No. I don't believe the official verdict of suicide. That was not my father's style.'

'Bloody hell. Look, Ronnie, I can definitely get you a brilliant deal on something in the area near your present place in Altea that's got an extra couple of bedrooms – and another brilliant deal on a sale of the present house. Leave all that to me. In the meantime, would you like to join me for a meal and a drink or two this evening? A pal of mine runs a nice, smart bar – the Segovia – near the common. Good food. And he'll let us have a private table upstairs. On me.'

In the light of Hazel's pregnancy, Ronnie Lewis had spent a good part of his holiday in Spain reflecting on the fruit-cake catastrophe and whether Sam the Stick was still worth bothering about, now that he had the much greater priority of approaching fatherhood.

Away from London, soothed by the sunshine and, at night, by holding Hazel in his arms, and relishing the prospect of being a father, Ronnie Lewis began to believe that, perhaps, he was not really suited to violent retribution, especially against a bed-ridden elderly man. Until, that is, his evening meal with William 'Big Bill' Crowe.

Eleven

The Segovia bar in Streatham was an ideal place for a secret assignation, whether it be a rendezvous between lovers, a meeting place for spies or, as in the case of Bill Crowe and Ronnie Lewis, two men plotting a mutually desired revenge. In the evening, the lighting on the upper floor, where Ronnie and Bill were dining and drinking in one of a few discreetly designed cubicles, was dimmed. And, should you approach or pass by the cubicle, you would catch only the barest word of the conversation within. The air was too loudly filled with sounds emanating from the crowded balcony bar – bottles being opened, glasses clinked, orders placed and complied with, voices raised in laughter or hoots of convivial disbelief: *What? Never! You didn't!* – all subsumed in a constant hum of chatter and unobtrusively melodic taped music.

In keeping with the atmosphere, Bill spoke in quiet tones. 'I'm assuming you're a chip off your father's block and ready for any plan that will bring us both the satisfaction due us,' he said, with a just-detectable note of menace in his voice.

'Of course,' Ronnie replied, by now inspired to shed his misgivings about Sam's unenviable state of health and, in Big Bill's company, to recover his sense of purpose in relation to the violent old villain who probably killed his father.

'I want to go to Spain and lead a new life free of unfinished business,' Ronnie said to his bulky companion. 'I want to clear it all up and not have to look back over my shoulder all the time.'

'So you're set on a clean break, then?'

'You bet. Hazel's arranging the conclusion of our lease on the flat in Clapham and Eddie has already got together a consortium of jazz-heads to buy the club. He is also helping me break up the gang. Most of Dad's old soldiers have already cut the strings. All on good terms. Nobody's unhappy. And I'm installing a manager in the shop in Acre Lane, leaving Eddie Lawrence to concentrate on music and looking after Jax. The new shop manager grew up in Brixton and now lives in Streatham. Knows the area. Decent feller with clean hands. But the thought of Sam the Stick getting away with it is still spoiling it all.'

'Why do you think Sam did it when the evidence points to suicide?'

'My father was not a man to commit suicide. He was no quitter. He was at a different stage of life than I am now with a young wife-to-be and a kid on the way. He, on the other hand, was established, confident, set to carry on for several more years. And not only did Sam Golub have a motive, but he was a vicious bastard and – funnily enough I kind of admire him for this – he was not someone to be afraid of hitting back.'

'Well, I don't admire him at all,' countered Big Bill. 'And, while it's good to know he's been brought down to the state of being shut up in a nursing home, I want him to be a bit more hurt. The care home is a matter of minutes from me so I propose that I take a look at the place, check the ways in and out, the general routine, so that we can get an idea of how we can get at him without being caught.'

'I already sent him a poisoned cake but… it didn't work.'

'Just as well. Poison can easily be traced back – if it's not detected in the cake or whatever in the first place, that is. That's a real risky thing to pull off. Let me recce the place. I obviously can't just walk up to the joint or drive there in my own identifiable motor. So I'll speak to my brother-in-law who rents out commercial vehicles. I'll tell him I want a vehicle to shift some boxes or something.'

A couple of weeks later, the two men met in Jax in the afternoon preceding a special Valentine's Night show. They found themselves in what used to be Little Jack's office where he handed out advice to his various petitioners, and had awaited Sam the Stick, 'wanting help with his mother's bills'.

Eddie Lawrence, and quite possibly Big Bill Crowe himself, knew that Sam had hoped for an audience with Little Jack but, Eddie had confirmed, 'he sadly chose the day upon which Little Jack decided to end it all.' Money troubles, Eddie suggested in a knowing voice to anyone who listened: 'Jack'd had a summons from the tax office regarding a somewhat large number of Her Majesty's pounds, and he was pissing himself about it.'

'Well,' Bill told Ronnie on that Valentine's afternoon, 'I duly drove up to Valley Ridge – quite a smart-looking place. There was a handy little side road alongside it, which looked like it led to another pathway at the back and all the way round the building. So I turned into it, and immediately found it was blocked off. Then I reversed out and drove away with a view to going back tomorrow and parking a short walking distance away in case I – or the van – had been recognised this morning.

'After I'd seen the barrier and stopped, a feller walking past, who looked like a truckie, called into the driving-seat window: "Yeah, mate, I made the same mistake myself earlier. It probably happens a lot. They should put a proper sign up to stop people doing that."

'"You're right there," I said, agreeing with the truckie, before reversing out sharpish into the road. By this time – it was still early morning – a few people were gathering, so I scarpered. I think it would be better to go on foot next time, maybe even tomorrow. I'll go to reception and ask if Mr Golub has any visitors, that I'm an old friend come to take him for a drive. Something along those lines. I'll think of some way of getting at him, don't you worry.

'In the meantime, I've found the perfect house for you and Hazel on the Costa Blanca, not far from your present gaff. My assistant Maria's dealing with it. She'll phone you in the morning. She can take you there next week for you to give it the once-over. But now, I've got to rush off to Portugal – the Algarve – to help some ex-con whose having trouble with his builders. Sounds like a long, drawn-out mess. So, by the next time I see you, you'll probably be the master of your very own new *casa*.'

And he shook Ronnie Lewis's hand. As he turned to go, Eddie Lawrence came running in, bursting to speak: 'Ronnie, Ronnie! Sam the Stick is dead. He was knocked down this morning by a van, just outside the care home.'

Ronnie didn't know whether to laugh or cry or merely express amazement. 'Bill, wait,' he said, holding back his visitor from leaving. Both men turned towards Eddie.

'That's a turn up for the books, eh, Eddie,' Bill Crowe said equivocally.

'A van,' Ronnie said, and paused before turning to Eddie: 'Would you mind leaving me and Bill alone for a few moments,' and, when Eddie had gone: 'You old dark horse! You did it. You sorted out Sam the Stick.'

'Not me,' said Bill.

'Oh, come on, stop playing.'

'I'm not playing. Wasn't me.'

'You paid someone else to do it?'

'No. Of course not. Look, I must rush. See you in Spain in a couple of months or so.'

'Come on, Bill, for God's sake. You got him. Stop messing around. Be serious.'

'I am always serious.'

And he was gone.

Twelve

On 14 February 1982, Benny wrote in his journal: 'Valentine's Day. What a time Sam chose to die – or be killed. A road accident or a hit-and-run? There is going to be a post-mortem to try and get a better idea of what happened. Crime or not, the little *lobbes* kept his sense of drama to the end. I'll miss him. I am so glad that I got to see him regularly in the care home before he died. We talked a lot about old times, something he'd always been reluctant to do. He even talked about the accident that permanently changed his life. It took him half a century to do that. But he spoke about it surprisingly eloquently.

'Only last week, he was joking about whether he was eligible for a place in the Guinness Book of Records, having spent so long in hospital or care-home beds both after the accident when he was twelve and more recently after falling off his ladder. And then, seemingly out of the blue, in a total change of mood, he said, "I feel bad about my old man."

'And when I asked him why, he recalled that his father "spent all those afternoons teaching me the Torah portion for my bar mitzvah as well as trying to keep up with what I should have been doing in school. He went to see old Wagman almost every week to find out what the class was up to and to borrow books. And one time he even brought Crazy Kaufman to the hospital to give me a lesson as I sat up in bed. You remember Mr Kaufman? Crazy

Kaufman," he said, "who tried to keep us interested in the lesson by telling jokes about famous writers and other historical figures but could never finish them because he always stammered as he got to the punchline? Did you know he was said to be the cleverest of all the teachers? I can't remember a word of that bedside lesson he gave me."

'I thought Sam was going to cry at one point – probably for the first time in those fifty years – as he related how he was only just realising how gentle and thoughtful his father had been towards him, whereas Sammy had always regarded him as strict, oppressive and even cruel to insist on teaching him while he was laid up in a hospital ward. And, possibly for the first time, he described how patiently his father went over the Hebrew words line by line. "I never appreciated any of it," he said. "I was just so angry about what had happened to my leg, angry with myself I suppose. And I was so rude and impatient with my poor old dad. I wish I could tell him now I'm sorry."

'Sam then swallowed hard and turned his head away briefly to one side, before beckoning me to sit closer to him. He leaned forward and whispered: "I also feel bad, very troubled that... I killed a man."

'I tried to reassure him. "A bastard," I said, "one of the deserving ones. You performed a heroic deed." He didn't say anything in answer to this but his face took on a very un-Sam-like expression, a kind of quiet acceptance, and he smiled softly as a father might smile apologetically to his child.

'And now, like his dad, and like Little Jack, Sam is gone.

'Bertha and I went see Joyce this afternoon. She looked exhausted but I sensed she was a little relieved. "I think I'm in shock," she said. "The tears won't come. What a sad and ridiculous way to die. Stupid. I feel angry and at the same time guilty that I couldn't manage to find a carer to look after him at home. But I couldn't have coped even if I had found one."'

Benny continued in the journal: 'It seems that Sam walked into a van reversing out of an old defunct service road adjoining the care home and was knocked down. Apparently, while he was reversing – quite rapidly – the driver of the van didn't see him or presumably even hear the sound of him being hit, and just continued backing out without noticing that Sam was lying flat on the ground in the old service track.

'Sam had still been taking early morning walks around the grounds of Valley Ridge and stopping to sit on the bench at the front of the building. The care home's management had ruled that Sam's regular walking route and Sam himself were both completely safe. The former service road had ceased to be used after a rear entrance and driveway were built a year ago and all deliveries went there. There was a barrier across the defunct route about twenty yards in. And no delivery was expected at that time of day anyway. The driver obviously had no connection to the nursing home and must have mistaken the service road for a proper turning and, when he realised his error, quickly reversed out.

'By the time the van driver had changed from reverse into a forward gear and begun to drive away along the street in the front of the Valley Ridge Nursing Home, Sam had painfully raised himself from the ground and tried to catch up with the moving vehicle.

'There were very few people about and not much traffic. The only witness, a cook who works at Valley Ridge, said the driver appeared momentarily to slow down but didn't stop. Sam threw his stick at the van before collapsing on the pavement. The stick somehow got caught in the van's rear bumper, and the momentum of the vehicle carried it along before dropping it about fifty yards from where Sam lay dying. The cook called for help and a receptionist at the home phoned for an ambulance but it was too late. Unless he was looking into his passenger-side wing mirror, the driver of the van quite possibly had no idea of what was happening on the pavement behind him.

'The cook said the driver had a cap on and she couldn't see his face properly. Nobody got the number of the van.'

Thirteen

Samuel Gideon Golub was buried in Marlow Road Cemetery in East London on 17 February 1982, three days after he died following the accident outside Valley Ridge Nursing Home in South London, and one day after a post-mortem verdict of accidental death was delivered. He had been a 'long-term care beneficiary' at Valley Ridge and, at sixty-two, one of its youngest residents.

His widow, Joyce Golub, decided not to hold a *shivah* service at home for her late husband but instead arranged with the authorities to have a memorial reception in the Valley Ridge function room and, a week later, with the help of Benny Pomeranski and Eddie Lawrence, a celebration of Sam's life at Jax jazz club in Richmond.

Joyce Golub's 'tears that wouldn't come' eventually flowed in the afternoon when she was getting ready for the reception at Valley Ridge.

Even though Sam hadn't been living in his and Joyce's house for several weeks, there were still, all over their home, many appurtenances of their life together and it was in contemplating some of these that Joyce found herself weeping.

His armchair, in which she hadn't sat since his admission to the care home, could not but convey a sense of his presence. And, going through a toolbox that contained an assortment of Sam's belongings, Joyce, smiling, picked out an old tin of a wax mixture for polishing walking sticks, among other wooden items. Sam had used this only once or twice in fifteen years but considered it a prized possession, perhaps because the tin bore the slogan: 'Used by the Gentry'.

Tucked behind a mirror on Joyce's dressing table was an old 'I'm sorry' letter from Sam to her, placed inside a large envelope which also contained, in their original little cloth bag, the 'Farringdon earrings' that he had kept for her throughout the period when they were apart.

Joyce had worn the earrings only once since their reconciliation but was planning to wear them at the jazz club celebration the following week. When she took them out of the envelope and read the letter again, her tears flowed copiously and moistened both the letter and the envelope.

On their bedroom wall was a very large printed copy, in the form of a poster mounted on cardboard, of Jack Elliott's lyrics to Lew Quadling's 'Sam's Song', bearing the signatures not only of Elliott and Quadling, but also of Dean Martin, who had performed and made a recording of 'Sam's Song' with Sammy Davis Junior.

Sam Golub had discovered the poster in a drawer when he was preparing to decorate the kitchen and stuck it on the wall alongside their bed. He'd found it in a charity shop many years earlier and bought it for less than five pounds. It had lain in the drawer ever since. Among other belongings, Joyce originally wanted to keep Sam's stick – the last remaining one – but it had been damaged in the course of the accident and was discarded.

A handful of Valley Ridge staff, including Daphne Hindhurst, the cook who witnessed Sam's last moments, came to the memorial reception, which was generally calm and sedate, and in which Joyce Golub found the kind of solace that she believed she would not have experienced in a traditional Jewish *shivah* prayer-gathering with all the attention upon her.

She also found Daphne Hindhurst to be a kind, caring woman, gracefully and sincerely apologetic for failing to take the licence number of the van that had struck Sam – 'I was much more concerned with getting him to hospital,' she recalled – but more for not having the first-aid or other skills that might have helped Sam feel comfortable at the end.

'You have no need to apologise,' Joyce told her. 'You did everything in your power to help, and made sure an ambulance was called almost immediately. You could not have done more.' To this, Daphne, her eyes filling, responded by holding the much smaller Joyce in an emotionally charged hug.

While Joyce Golub said that the memorial reception made her feel 'serene', Benny Pomeranski described the celebration that followed a week later as 'so upbeat it was joyous'. It attracted a big crowd – 'Jax is full to the max' was Eddie Lawrence's comment. Along with his own quartet, 'Eddie's Reddies', he had booked 'local singing sensation' Estelle Davis and (at Estelle's request) her actress daughter, Gloria, over from her home in the United States. Benny, Bertha and Renée Lewis helped to make sure there was enough food and Eddie Lawrence looked after the drink.

It was billed as a celebration, and that was just how it turned out. For a man who had often been feared or loathed for his short temper and aggressive manner, the atmosphere was remarkably warm and affectionate throughout, full of laughter, noise and memories. Towards the end, Gloria Davis read out some words that Joyce had cobbled together about Sam, and Simon Pomeranski followed, reading his father Benny's equally touching tribute to 'the Stick'. The two readers then took a joint bow and warmly hugged each other.

Although Gloria had enjoyed cumulative success as an actress in America – on stage, television and latterly the cinema screen – she and Simon both retained fond memories of her beginnings in Blackheath, to where her mother had been instrumental in sending her.

After Gloria had left school, she helped Estelle with bookings, travel and singing practice for a couple of years, then drifted somewhat before living with a boyfriend who earned a small living putting on rock music concerts for students, and a slightly larger living from trading in marijuana. Eventually, Estelle persuaded Fancy Goods Harry's wife, Celia, who was an amateur dramatics enthusiast, to give Gloria a minor part in a show her company was putting on.

From that moment, Gloria was hooked. She was determined to go on the stage and Estelle helped out again by sending her to Simon Pomeranski, who by then was combining directing with teaching. He was immediately impressed and agreed to take her on after a single session. After three or four lessons, when she came home singing Simon's praises, Estelle exclaimed, 'Oh no, look out. Slow down. You're not making a move for Simon Pomeranski, are you?'

'Are you kidding,' Gloria replied. 'He is head-over-heels for Marina Lawson. She and Edward Lowden are Simon's twin shining lights. Ed's got a contract with the RSC and Marina's been signed up for a BBC TV costume drama – Jane Austen, I think.'

Soon after that exchange, Gloria left Simon's class for New York, where a friend had a connection with an off-Broadway theatre group. It was a slow start for Gloria but within eighteen months she was starring in a production of Tennessee Williams's play, *A Streetcar Named Desire*. Then all the barriers fell down and she was on her way.

The whole remembrance in honour of Sam the Stick, the impact of which lasted from the start of the reception at Valley Ridge to the close of the party at Jax, was an outstanding success – with an ironic aspect in the case of the Jax event.

Early in the week, between the reception and the celebration, Benny had tracked down Eddie in his office. 'Does Ronnie Lewis know we're planning this event on Saturday night?' Benny asked, once Eddie had poured him a whisky.

'Well,' said Eddie, 'you probably know that Ronnie's in Spain at the moment but obviously we had to get his permission. You know what he said? "If people want to celebrate the fact that Sam the Stick is dead, I'm all for it. It's like dancing on his grave."'

'What a jerk,' Benny responded.

Eddie nodded in a contemplative manner and said, 'Ronnie is not the brightest of men, Benny. You must know that. And he's naïve. And impressionable. Not long ago, I convinced him that I was an expert in poisons. What would I know about a thing like that? The nearest I've ever got to poisoning was sucking my own spittle off the mouthpiece of my clarinet.'

Benny didn't laugh but fixed Eddie with a penetrating stare and asked, in a slow and carefully enunciated manner, 'Eddie, are you by any chance telling me that Ronnie Lewis tried to poison Sam and asked you to advise him how to do it?'

'No, Benny,' Eddie retorted with equally careful enunciation. 'I am not telling you that.'

'Because,' a now-sceptical Benny said, 'a cake, ostensibly from Sam's brother who hadn't spoken to him for years, was sent to Sam, who worried that it might have been got at. He had given it to his friend George in Valley Ridge, who did suddenly die, as it happens. It looked suspicious but they carried out a post-mortem and it seems to have been nothing to do with the cake.

'George was suffering from pneumonia and no one realised how severe it was because he'd just carried on as normal. He was quite something, that man. He had managed to endure much more than a bout of old-age pneumonia in a cosy South London nursing home. I'm still surprised that he succumbed to it. And it's still a bit of a coincidence about the cake and now you mentioning poison.'

'Ronnie asks me about all sorts of crazy things,' Eddie said. 'And if I tell him, "Oh I know all about that," it's the quickest way to end the subject and prevent him probing. He's not only asked me about poison but also about guns and knives and stuff. What do I know about any of it? I'm just a little old jazzman. But I know how to play discord. You can serve up fakes all day long to a man like Ronnie Lewis and he won't notice.'

'As it happens,' Benny repeated, 'Sam's brother died soon after he would have sent the cake. So, now, Sam's brother Dave has died, his friend George in the care home has died, Sam himself has died – and Little Jack is dead, too.'

'Are *you* now telling *me*, Benny, by any chance, that Sam killed Little Jack?'

'No, Eddie, I am not telling you that.'

And both men smiled and shook hands.

The Samuel Golub memorial celebration ended with Estelle Davis calling her daughter to join her on stage in a duet version of 'It Was Just One of Those Things' backed by Eddie's Reddies. The duo then elided into 'Sam's Song' and Gloria held up the board with Jack Elliott's lyrics reproduced on it, which Joyce had brought from home, and invited everyone, sitting, standing or dancing, to join in.

Benny Pomeranski was just about the only person who didn't join in. He'd been too shaken by Estelle's choice, for the previous song, of Cole Porter's matchless reflection on the end of an affair:

If we'd thought a bit
Of the end of it
When we started painting the town
We'd have been aware
That our love affair
Was too hot not to cool down

Fourteen

BD: Come on, Bill, you recognise me. Your old shipmate.
CAPTAIN: (turns abruptly and fearfully, hand on his cutlass) Black Dog!
BD (smiles menacingly): The very same. Black Dog come to the Admiral Benbow inn to see his old shipmate, Bill. Ah, Bill, Bill. We have seen such sights and times, we two, set sail and back again in the company of death.
CAPTAIN: It is company in which you seem most to delight.

FROM *TREASURE ISLAND* BY ROBERT LOUIS STEVENSON, ADAPTED FOR THE STAGE BY SIMON POMERANSKI

'A coloured man.'
'Oh, a coloured man, you say?'
'Yeah, that's right. About two or three inches taller than me. Haven't seen him in a long time, so don't know exactly what he looks like now. But I've got a photograph of him when he was young and in his prime. Here you are, look.'
'A boxer, eh? Don't get too many boxers round hereabouts.'
'This was taken a long time ago. He'd be much older now, and I doubt he still carries any kind of punch.'

Des Lynch had been the landlord of the Seafarer Hotel and Bar in County Mayo for nearly forty years. It had been a steady, reliable business, a loyal bunch of locals leavened by a healthy flow of tourists saw to that. But, of late, his formerly quiet coastal retreat had been boosted by a couple of enthusiastic reviews in national publications and Des found himself having to adapt to an influx of a more varied range of customers.

In keeping with this trend, Mister Jeffrey Calloway, currently staying alone in the Seafarer's 'Ocean Suite', stood out on account of his slow, measured way of talking, and his constant references, delivered in a soft, Caribbean-tinged London accent, to how the Seafarer had 'changed out of all recognition' since he had been brought there for childhood holidays.

And now, while not so exotic as Mr Calloway, here was another singular individual, asking not for room and board but for information 'about an old friend of mine. I haven't seen him in years. I was told he was coming over to Mayo for a visit but I don't know which hotel or boarding house he's staying at. He's a few years older than me. I was wondering if he's staying here.'

Des eyed the stranger with more than a modicum of suspicion and asked him where he was from.

'London, just like my friend. We practically grew up together. In the same house. Though he's quite a bit older than I am,' the stranger repeated. The age difference seemed to matter to him.

'And he's a boxer?'

'Used to be. Yeah.'

'Are you from the police?'

'That's a laugh. Nah.'

'And what's your friend's name?'

'He goes by different names. When I was a kid I knew him as Joey. I looked up to him. He was a top fighter. Have a closer look at that photo. You can see a "J" printed on his shorts. His full name was Joseph Campbell.'

'And what may be your name, sir?'

'Ronnie. Ronnie Lewis. If you are able to locate him here in your fine hotel, please tell him I am the son of Little Jack.'

'Little Jack, you say?'

'That is correct.'

'Sounds like a man of the sea. He'd likely feel at home in our establishment – the Seafarer.'

'He's no longer of the sea or the sky.' The garrulous Des Lynch appeared to have unlocked an unlikely poetic note within Ronnie Lewis's gruff vocabulary.

'Sadly my father passed away,' Ronnie went on. 'And he liked to operate on dry land rather than water.'

'Well, we all have to make our way over the land in one way or another, and most of us are destined to lie beneath it.'

'Yes we are, but for now please let me know if my friend is staying under your roof.'

'Of course. Please take a seat, Mr Lewis, over there in the bar, and I'll take a look through the bookings.'

'Can't you just check your guest list?'

'I don't have a Mr Campbell here at the moment, sir. Neither, as far as I know, do I have a Joseph. But let me check. You just make yourself comfortable. Get yourself a drink. I shouldn't be long.'

Ronnie Lewis gave a shrug and went through to the bar. He ordered a Jameson's and sat in an armchair from where he could see (and be seen) through the glass door to the reception.

Des Lynch, meanwhile, called his son, Danny – who assisted him in managing the Seafarer – from his office in an anteroom behind the reception area. Des did not trust Ronnie Lewis and thought it prudent to have his big, strapping and combative offspring near. He told Danny that the stranger sitting in the bar knocking back whiskey was snooping around asking for the whereabouts of a man, a former boxer, who, from the stranger's description, sounded very much like Mr Calloway in the Ocean Suite.

'Please go and see if Calloway's there,' Des quietly told his son, 'and, if he is, tell him there's a Mr Ronnie Lewis in reception asking about a long-lost friend who used to be a boxer but this Lewis fellow doesn't seem to be too certain about the man's name. He thinks it's Joey. And this Ronnie Lewis is, he says, the son of "Little Jack". If Calloway knows Lewis and is happy to see him, fine. Take him through to the bar. If not, I'll tell Lewis sorry we're unable to help. Oh, and check with Robbie at the bar that the bugger's paid for his drink.'

Two or three minutes later, Danny was back. 'It's okay,' he said. 'Ronnie Lewis is on the level. Our guest knows him. I told him that his visitor thought his name was Joey. "I used to be called that," he answers, "but no more." I'll send our feller in the bar through to your man, for that's what he asked. He didn't want to come out to meet his little fan.'

Ronnie had sunk his Jameson's and was emitting a satisfied breath when Danny appeared in the bar. 'I've found your gentleman,' said the younger Lynch. 'He recognised your name and, though he is registered here as Mr Jeffrey Calloway, he did say that he used to be known by his nickname, Joey, and his mum's surname. I thought he might be your friend, seeing as how he is the only coloured man among our guests at present. If the name you gave had been the same as what he checked in as – and which was on his passport – we could have helped you much quicker. Come with me and I'll take you to him. He's staying in our special suite so you can sit together and chat in his lounge area without being disturbed. Follow me, sir.'

Aaron 'Ronnie' Lewis stood up, arranged his face into what he hoped was a determined and menacing expression, and walked briskly through the bar door that Danny Lynch was holding open for him. Danny's face was somewhat more easily arranged into a smile as he tapped on the door to the Ocean Suite.

Fifteen

Sometimes, when Benny was at his most introspective in his journal, Simon found it too difficult to read. The bulk of the journal's content carried no overt indication of a desire for publication but, often, the careful structure, the occasional artifice, the obvious delight in writing and the power of individual words used by Benny indicated a need not just to get things off his chest, but to address directly an imagined reader or readers, whether within the family or wider-ranging.

Elsewhere, however, the subject matter – mostly towards the end – seemed to have simply spilled out of Benny Pomeranski's mind unchecked, the handwriting rushed and barely legible. The impressive discipline of most of the journal's material appeared to have been abandoned, without a thought for its clarity. Or indeed for its propriety. Here, his motive was clearly neither to demonstrate or solicit praise for his communicative powers, but seemingly just to be well thought of, understood, remembered as an honest man who *owned up*. And, where there still could be detected a voice addressing the reader, its tone took on a deeply confidential air.

Nevertheless, especially in the later pages, Simon sometimes found himself confronted by material so personal that, despite his sense of the journal as a whole posthumously facilitating a bond between father and son, he felt he was intruding into an area that belonged only to his father. And, having stumbled into such territory, he would – at least on the initial encounter – skip several paragraphs, or even pages, thereby avoiding, for example, Benny's raw, sometimes barely coherent brooding, in overpoweringly physical detail, on the uneasy combinations of debilitating guilt and exhilarating pleasure, oppressive sadness and liberating joy, derived from his relationship with Estelle.

Leaving aside Benny's quotations from press coverage of Ruth Ellis, his journal entries dedicated to Estelle tended to be the longest. But the most words overall – boosted by many short and passing mentions – were devoted to Sam Golub. More even than those about Bertha, Benny's wife of over half a century, or his son, Simon.

It would be hard to think of two people so unlike each other as Benjamin Pomeranski and Samuel Golub and yet they remained bound together through the history of a shared childhood and adolescence, the geography of movement from east to south, the society of the Astorian crew, and the trauma – through Sam's 'accidents' – of a maiming, on one London street, exacerbated in a domestic setting, and carried to its fateful conclusion on another.

Occasionally, Benny wrote that, in some ways, he envied Sam. For Sam was bold and fearless, where Benny described himself as cowardly. Sam was genuinely decisive where Benny only pretended to be. 'The more I boasted, the more I displayed my weakness,' is how Benny summed this up towards the end of the journal.

'I even shamefully envied Sam's brief but uplifting friendship at the end with George Cowan in the care home,' he said, 'and, even worse, I slightly envied dear old George for the sheer *distinction* of being a Holocaust survivor and, as such, being able to look death in the face and treat it with contempt.'

Sixteen

As he held open the door of the Ocean Suite to allow Jeff Calloway to greet his visitor, Danny Lynch made the introduction: 'Mr Calloway, here is Mr Lewis to see you. Will that be all?'

'Yes thank you,' said Jeff as he stood up from the sofa.

'Just call the desk if you need anything.'

'I will, thanks.'

And Danny was gone.

'So, Aaron Lewis, the kid I used to teach to shadow-box. Sit down. It's been a long time. Is it really you?'

'It definitely is me – which is more than you could say for yourself, Joseph Campbell.'

'Ah yes, I've moved on since then.'

'How so?'

'I'd long wanted to trace back my roots...'

'Long wanted? You'd done all right as you were in London. Top fighter. Loads of money...'

'Not as much as you might think, actually, but yes, I was comfortable enough. But I *had* long wanted to dig back into my dad's Jamaican roots and maybe locate some of his family. I was curious. And once I started getting plagued by the press and all that, people pointing me out in the street, I was desperate to get away and be anonymous and not allow myself to be forced into continuing in a career where I could end up an old geezer with cauliflower ears, a broken nose and beaten-up face.'

'But you pissed off in a bit of a sudden rush.'

'Well, there was a chance of an early boat booking…'

'And a change of name.'

'Yeah, there was a once-in-a-lifetime chance of putting all these things together. I had to race away after the Butch Martin fight. I'd had enough of the fight game. And it was such a relief, a pleasure, in Jamaica not to keep being recognised in the street…'

'I bet it was,' Ronnie sneered.

'Yes it really was, as a matter of fact. The nearest it got was the odd remark – "Hey, you remind me of somebody, a boxer," or even one time, "a singer" – and even that faded away over the years. I loved it and decided to stay.'

'Yes, but you ran away without saying goodbye to anyone it seems. Most of all, to my father, who had taken you under his wing when you were a little rough-house orphan kid. And set you on your way.'

'I was not an orphan. My dad left us when I was two or three and my mum couldn't cope. I believe my father died in America or Jamaica. I never found out exactly. I did try to in Jamaica but couldn't find any clues. And, to tell you the truth, I lost interest in the old bastard. After all, he didn't bother with me or my mum. My identity has been for a long time, and now always will remain, Jeffrey Calloway.'

Jeff's face tightened as he surveyed the would-be replica of Little Jack Lewis sitting opposite him. 'Do you want a cup of coffee?' Jeff said, still training his eyes on Ronnie. 'I've got coffee here in the room. Why don't you take your coat off? Are you cold? It's actually a warm room.'

'Yeah, I am a bit. But I'm warming up. And coffee would be great. Thanks.'

'How and why did you come to see me here?' Jeff asked as he put the now-filled cup on to a coffee table in front of the chair where his unexpected visitor was sitting.

Ronnie bent the truth a little at this point. He was not yet in a position to tell his potential victim that he had been trailing him for quite a while. 'Oh, I told my mother I wanted to visit Ireland,' he said. 'And she mentioned that she'd heard you came regularly to this part, to Mayo, and so I thought, while I was here, I'd look you up on the off chance.

'This is only the second hotel I've tried. I knew you'd be in a smart one,' Ronnie added, and then asked: 'You mind if I smoke?'

'No, that's fine. There's an ashtray on the table.'

'Ta, d'you want a fag?'

'No thanks. I haven't had a cigarette since I moved out of your place in Streatham.'

'Yeah, the house where you tried to rape my mother.'

In the ten seconds of silence that followed, Ronnie almost sucked his cigarette into his mouth as he inhaled dramatically, his eyes fixed on Jeff's face.

'Who told you that?'

'I just know what goes on all around Brixton. Just like my father, my late father, did.'

'Late father? Yeah, I heard Little Jack was dead. Is that why you've been trying to find me? On account of some bastard's shitty little lie about me trying to rape your mum?'

'It's a lie, is it?' Ronnie, who had been sitting close to the edge of his chair, moved forward even more to tap some ash into the ashtray. At the same time, Jeff was mentally estimating how long it would take Ronnie to stretch forward to place his cigarette end in the ashtray, pour the remains of his coffee down his throat, put down the cup and move his hand away from the table.

Which is precisely what Ronnie did before standing up. Jeff, too, stood up, a flicker of a second before Ronnie could reach into the slightly bulging right-hand pocket of his coat.

The 'Kid' had always had lightning-fast reflexes and they still held up in his later years. He reached Ronnie's side in an instant, pulling the would-be gangster's right arm up and away from his pocket, from which Jeff relieved him of a Glock slimline handgun taped into a couple of brown paper bags.

'Very classy, Ronnie.' Jeff laughed at his own sarcasm. 'You just get back on that chair,' he said, pointing a finger. Ronnie instantly obeyed, almost falling on the chair as the blood drained from his face. 'Trying to be the big shot like your dad, eh? You saw him at even closer quarters than I did. Unless you are stupid or blind you must have realised that he didn't exactly set a good example.'

Ronnie couldn't stop shaking and breathing heavily, blowing out his cheeks. After one particularly long exhalation, he nervously managed to speak in a soft and broken voice: 'I looked up to my father. He was a strong man. He wouldn't take any shit from anybody.'

'That's because he didn't need any. He was total shit himself. No room for any more. Eh, young Aaron? I'm amazed you haven't worked this out for yourself but I hate to tell you: your old man was a thoroughly nasty piece of work, far worse than anyone I've encountered in the boxing world.'

'Is that what you thought? Is that why you ran away. Scared of what he might do to you after he'd found out about you and Mum?'

'Little Jack wouldn't *do* anything. He paid others – better armed than you are – to do things for him. Can you imagine a straight confrontation between him and me? No weapons, no gloves. I'd have knocked his fucking head off his shoulders. And you need to get it into *your* head that there was nothing going on between your mother and me. Did you bother to ask her?'

'I was...'

'Too scared?'

'Too embarrassed, ashamed.'

'Ashamed? Who of? Yourself? Your dad? Surely not your mum, dear old Renée. She deserved better than him. Now, listen,' Jeff continued firmly. 'I've got a hire car arriving for me any minute. I've planned for myself a drive to see some of the County Mayo coastline that I knew when I was a kid. And I'm not letting you put me off. You are coming with me, Ronnie. It'll do you good. You can drive. I'll sit in the back keeping an eye on you.'

'Please don't sit behind me. Please don't shoot me in the head!'

'Keep the noise down. We don't want Mine Host or his big boy-child coming to find out what's going on and for them and me to turn you in to the police, do we? Threatening me with a, presumably illegal, deadly weapon. And I like sitting in the back. I'll have a better view. And, once we get going, I'll navigate. And you will do as you are told. If you so much as twitch, I'll stick your little pea-shooter gun up one of your nostrils and give your nasal hair a bit of a singe.'

At that moment, Des Lynch rang from reception to tell 'Mr Calloway' that his hire car had arrived. 'Right on the button,' Jeff said with a smirk directed at Ronnie Lewis. 'You can sit in the vehicle while I deal with the formalities. Your little weapon is now in my pocket and my fingers will never be more than an inch and a half from the trigger. So just relax. It'll be nice to have some company.'

And so the two men embarked on the unlikeliest of tourist excursions. Jeff directed Ronnie to Portacloy Beach on the very edge of the land, where they parked the car and got out to take the local 'Loop Cliff' walk. The weather was clear and mild, warm for the time of year, and the route had minimal out-of-season traffic.

Ronnie had relaxed a little as he drove along the Irish country roads and listened to Jeff telling him about the uncompleted deal to fix the Butch Martin fight from which Little Jack stood to gain a large lump sum. And how he'd thought it prudent to make a rapid break abroad, to the land of his fathers, 'where I always wanted to go, more than I wanted to come to Ireland, where I lived for the first few years of my life before my ma left for London with me, hoping to get some help in bringing me up. I could only recall the holidays when I was a kid here. It seemed like coming to heaven compared to where I was in care in South London.'

'So you had a motive for killing my father,' Ronnie said, gathering confidence, after he'd parked the car and they began their cliff-top stroll.

'A lot of people had a motive for doing away with your dear daddy.'

'Can you blame me for wanting to equalise my father's murder?'

'Not if it *was* murder and I had done it. But your dad shot himself. And, in the very unlikely event of his having been killed by somebody, it certainly wasn't me. That is not my style.'

'Why would he shoot himself? He had a good life.'

'Depends on what you mean by "good".'

'He was strong, successful, with a good home and two children. He certainly wasn't a coward. If anything was wrong, he would have sorted it out. As he would have done with your double-crossing him if you hadn't sprinted away so fast... I *know* he was killed.'

'Well, you can't really know, especially if you are accusing me, because I *know* I didn't do it.'

'I'm not actually accusing you directly. You are one of two suspects.'

At this point they had come to a small copse where they were hidden from the view of the very few people out and about.

'Let's stop here a minute,' said Jeff. 'Isn't it beautiful! Makes you feel lucky to be alive, don't you think, young Aaron?' Ronnie Lewis's response to this goading was an absent-minded shrug of indifference and a desperate gulp in the throat. 'So, *two* suspects,' Jeff Calloway continued.

'Yes. My father was killed either by you or Sam Golub, and I can't sleep until I make good. My dad always paid his debts.'

'And so you were after my hide? Have you now ruled out Sam?'

'No. I think he was the more likely but you had such a strong motive – fear. And even stronger, I can now see, since you cheated on him by not throwing the fight.'

'Well, the situation has changed now. Now I have the gun and you are the easy target. Nobody could hear anything from here, or even necessarily see anything being tossed off the cliff in the fading light. Which is what I am intending to do.'

'No! Please! I beg you. Don't make my child an orphan before he's born. You've persuaded me it wasn't you. And you weren't around. I wasn't going to shoot you. I just wanted to find out more about your whereabouts and whether you knew about Sam Golub having done it. Please! I'm begging you.'

'Look at you. Mr Big of South London, pissing your pants. You could do with a swim to cover up that little patch leaking into your trousers. Maybe starting with a high dive from the cliffs, eh?' And Jeff swiftly pulled the gun from his pocket, still wrapped in one of the paper bags.

'Please don't kill me. My girlfriend and I are planning to turn our backs on our life in London, which I'm finding harder and harder,' pleaded Ronnie, who had fallen on his knees. 'She's called Hazel. She's a few years younger than me – and we're having a baby. She's pregnant. And she is lovely. She is good for me, helping me to be a better person. My mum and sister say she's too good for me and,' he said, slowing down, 'I think maybe they're right.'

'They almost certainly are. Now, be quiet. Get up and follow me.'

Jeff signalled to Ronnie to come out of the copse, and held the covered weapon close-up between the terrified Ronnie's eyes before hurling it into the waters below and calmly telling the wet-trousered Ronnie Lewis: 'Your father was not someone to look up to. A nasty human being but, for all that, I wouldn't have killed him. Believe me, it is always better to spare a life than to take it. I feel much better for sparing yours than finishing it, even though you were apparently planning to shoot me.'

'I couldn't have done it,' Ronnie said, panting rapidly. 'When it comes to it, I don't have the courage. I just wanted to see my father's killer scared and begging for mercy.'

'And is that what you're planning for Sam and his stick? He won't let you get away with that. He is a vicious man.'

'He's dead.'

'Really? By your hand?'

'No.'

'Well I'm blown. I had no idea. Poor old Sam. I always thought of him as a dear old sheep in wolf's clothing. Come on, Piss-Pants. You can drive me back. I'll sit next to you this time. And I'll thank you to take yourself off home as soon as we get there. Do you have a car parked at the hotel?'

'Yes.'

'Ha! We could have taken that and saved on the hire fee. Where do you live?'

'Clapham, though I have a place in Spain and my girlfriend and me want to live there eventually. I'm catching the Cork ferry to Swansea first thing in the morning. Then it's back to London. I'm driving to Cork and stopping overnight.'

'Clapham, eh? I know Clapham quite well.'

The two men barely spoke on the journey back to the Seafarers Inn, except when Ronnie suddenly braked by the side of the road and sobbed almost as profusely as he had urinated earlier. 'I'm sorry,' he hiccoughed. 'It's just that I feel so relieved. To be alive. Not to be killed.'

His voice sounded like that of a child. Jeff handed him the large box of tissues that was placed in the back of the hire car. 'Here,' Jeff said. 'And you might want to use one or two tissues on your pants. And your prick, as well. And on the car seat in case any little bit has seeped through.'

Back at the gates of the hotel, as they parted, Jeff told his chastened would-be assassin, 'I hope you have a fair crossing and a good journey home. I want you to think about how we both refrained from pulling the trigger. I definitely did and I believe what you say about not being able to do it. That's not cowardice. It's a much higher thing. The right thing. Now we both have lives to live. Distant lives. All I want to say is that I haven't thought anything – good or bad – of your father for many years. He wasn't worth it. And now, I – and we, the rest of us in our little Astorian group – will think no further of you.'

Seventeen

In September 2001, a Jewish friend of Estelle Davis's, with whom she was chatting in the street, happened to mention that, on the following day, a Sunday, she was going to visit the tomb of her brother who had died in a car crash a few years earlier.

'Will you be taking flowers?' Estelle asked.

'No, no, not flowers,' her friend answered, 'I always place a stone on his grave.'

'A stone? Why?'

'I'm not sure, but it always makes me feel good – that I am making a connection to him. And visitors to his grave can see by the stones that others have been to pay their respects. It's a tradition. I think it's to do with the stone's indestructibility – unlike flowers. And this is the time of the year, the Jewish New Year is coming up, when we visit our loved ones' graves. My parents', too, but especially Adrian's. They lived long lives but he died far too young. We were very close.'

After she and her friend had parted, Estelle returned to her flat with a plan forming in her head. The next day, she decided, she would go to a cemetery, but not the one her friend was visiting.

It was quite crowded when she arrived. The weather was perfect – a warm sun and a cool breeze – so different from the November of the previous year when Benjamin Pomeranski was lowered into his last resting place there. She saw stones on many of the graves, and some people placing fresh ones.

She took a while to locate Benny's plot. It irreverently brought to mind trying to find a car among many others in a car park. Then, as she eventually approached it, she could see a woman in a headscarf bending down alongside the grave. A woman last seen by Estelle Davis at Benny's funeral. Too late to stop now.

'Bertha, hello.'

'Oh, it's you.'

'Yes, it's me. I wish you long life.'

'Thank you. I never expected to see you here.'

'I didn't expect to see you. I'm sorry, I should have thought. It's the Jewish New Year. Sorry if I've disturbed you. I just felt that I wanted to come. Ought to. I was too miserable at the funeral to... pay my respects.'

'It's nice of you to come,' said Bertha standing up.

'I thought you would be angry.'

'No. It's actually comforting that I'm not alone in missing him – me and my son Simon, of course. As it happens, I was thinking of writing to you.'

'Really? I was thinking the same. I wanted to make contact with you.'

'Maybe we should meet for a coffee some day. Somewhere other than the cemetery. Or,' she said emphatically, 'the Astoria café.' And she smiled for the first time.

And Estelle smiled back. 'Oh, that's been closed for many years.' A difficult moment of silence was then broken by Estelle, looking down at the grave: 'It looks a lot different from the day of the funeral. It looks and feels better with the tombstone, the nice wording, and of course it is so much quieter today.'

'Yes,' said Bertha. 'I think it's a fine stone. People tend nowadays to wait twelve months after the burial to set the tombstone but we had it done after six months.'

This time Bertha broke the ensuing silence. She looked away before asking: 'How did you feel when it ended?'

'I was devastated. I felt he gave me so much. A kind of education.'

'Education? He was no college professor.'

'For sure, but there was something that he had, a knack of communicating what was important. And he knew a lot, above and beyond the dresses and Brixton and the Astoria boys.'

'I know. He certainly loved his books and his music.'

'And he loved you. I asked him, straight up, when we first met, and he said "yes" unhesitatingly.'

'I am sure he loved both of us. You were his passion. And I like to think I was his rock. I could have killed him when I found out about your affair, but I think I slowly accommodated you – or the idea of you – into our lives. And that's the point, it was still *our* lives, Benny's and mine.'

'I know and that was what mattered most. I kind of knew, at the back of my mind, that he would have to end our relationship one day. And, when he did, my knowing it had to happen, that it was inevitable, kind of cushioned the blow. Made me wake up and stop dreaming. As he said: "Sooner or later we all have to face reality." And that's a good thing.

'On the other hand,' Estelle continued, 'I did for some time think he and I would get together permanently at some stage and I believed that he thought the same. So at first I *was* devastated. Completely shattered and angry. And, above all, disillusioned. Disillusioned because I imagined we were for all time and suddenly realised that he, deep down, can't have imagined that in the same way. So I suffered what I thought was a big loss. I had terrible mood swings and, at my worst, I was so angry at myself for having wasted all that time. But then,' Estelle resumed after a deep breath, 'I realised it wasn't at all a waste of time. It did me good.'

'And now,' Bertha said, 'I am forced to say it, I admit that you did him good. You softened him. When we moved to Brixton after the war, he was so excited playing cops and robbers with Sam and sad old Maxie and the others, and of course the disgusting *Little Jack*' – she uttered the two words with stinging contempt – 'and spoke a lot of nonsense describing what was nothing more than petty thieving and threatening people as a sort of political stance. A philosophy.

'Even though he'd been in the war, in action in the Middle East,' Bertha recalled, 'I still thought of him as little more than a kid. What drove him most in those days – him and Sam certainly – was handing out meaningful paybacks. They took great pleasure in taking big shots and rich bosses down a peg or two. And Sam, in particular, got great satisfaction in dishing out what he – and Benny but especially Sam – saw as justice.'

By now, the two women had slowly walked about fifty yards from Benny's grave towards a bench, where Bertha suggested they sit down. And she immediately resumed speaking: 'One day, when we weren't yet married and were still living in the East End, his dad gave him a few quid to get measured for a new suit at Sid Sugarman's in Vallance Road.

'He couldn't wait to collect it the minute it was made up. And, when he did, he put it on straight away and sauntered his way home like a peacock. The next day, he was walking along Brick Lane, wearing the new suit with a white shirt and one of his dad's ties, thinking he was *it*.

'In those days,' she continued, 'there was a young bloke in our area called Issy Greenstein – have you heard of him? No? A huge, rough individual with nothing much between the ears. In fact, he was what used to be called ESN, "educationally sub-normal". And he was a bully. His father once got him into a boxing club and when he had his first bout – it was against another unusually big Yiddishe boy from a rival club in Stepney – Issy's two brothers went along to cheer on his opponent!

'Anyway, this Issy Greenstein and one of his mates happen to be coming down Brick Lane as Benny, in full swagger in his smart new suit, is walking in the opposite direction. Issy and his mate start laughing and taking the P out of Benny. Benny says: "Leave me alone, you big lump." Then Issy pushes him against the wall and grabs the lapels of his new suit while Issy's mate scoops up some mud from the recently rained-on kerb and rubs it on Benny's sleeve.

'Benny then tries to push the pair away and Issy says: "Oh, you wanna fight, do yer?" And he and his mate force Benny along the pavement towards a bombsite just off Brick Lane so they can give him a good hiding.

'As they turn off the road into the short alley leading to the bombsite, Benny relaxes into Issy's grip, smiles and gives a little laugh – which really gets Issy going. "Oh, so you think I'm funny do you?" he says. "You need to be taught a lesson." And he drags Benny out of sight from the main road and begins his "lesson" with a violent back-hander across Benny's face.

'By this time, they are on the edge of the bombsite. And there, standing no more than a yard or two from them, is Sam, along with lanky Harry Miller – long before his fancy goods days – and two tough local brothers, Jonny and Jack Fairman, friends more of Sam's than Benny's but still matey and who, what's more, used to go regularly to that bombsite to run across the uneven ground as part of a football training routine. Two strong, fit boys.

'What Issy Greenstein didn't know was that Benny had been on the way to meet Sam and the others when he'd been picked on by Issy and his mate and led, fortuitously, towards their meeting place.

'Issy's mud-throwing mate immediately turns on his heels and runs. Issy goes as if to run but is tripped by Benny, whereupon the other lads leap on Issy and inflict multiple injuries to his face, ribs and hands.

'When they'd gone, Issy Greenstein, after what I imagine must have been a few very painful attempts, got as far as the pavement on Brick Lane and passed out. After a while, an ambulance came and took him to hospital. For the next few days, Benny was walking on air. "Justice triumphed," he kept saying to me. He knew that neither Issy nor his little accomplice would ever tell the police and, having himself landed a few telling blows to the bully's nose and chin, he felt fulfilled.

'Benny was so pumped up,' Bertha went on, 'I was worried that he would go on to lead a violent criminal life mixing with thugs and undesirables but he seemed to think beating up Issy – giving a bully, even one who was a bit mentally backward, a taste of his own medicine – was a totally moral thing.'

'Getting your own back is such a gut thing,' Estelle commented. 'Satisfying. "Elemental," Benny would say.'

'Yes,' said Bertha with a laugh, 'he often used that word.'

'I think it was you not me that softened him up,' Estelle said.

'Actually, I think he was always a softy at heart,' said Bertha.

'Yes,' Estelle agreed, allowing her whole face to smile gently.

'Let's go and bid him goodbye shall we,' said Bertha, inclining her head in the direction of the remains of Benjamin Emanuel Pomeranski – 'A man of intelligence, resource and kindness' according to the words recently inscribed on his tombstone. 'Loved and warmly remembered by his wife Bertha, son Simon, daughter-in-law Marina, and grandsons, Will and Jonathan'.

At the graveside, the two women stopped, and hugged each other. Estelle then bent down and picked up a stone, which she placed next to Bertha's.

Epilogue

BERTHA POMERANSKI sold the Pomeranski Gowns business shortly after Benny Pomeranski's death. Which is what she and Benny had intended to do until he became ill six weeks before he died. When Bertha was halfway through negotiations with a menswear chain, 'Spanish' Joe Pelovsky and Ralph Landau, by then business as well as life partners, intervened with a higher bid, which Bertha accepted. After Benny's death, Bertha's sister Louise moved out of her home in Waltham Abbey and came to live with Bertha in her flat in Highgate. Bertha died aged eighty-eight in 2009. Louise, her 'frail, sickly' sister, two years Bertha's junior, outlived her by nine years.

ESTELLE DAVIS continued to sing professionally into her late sixties, but was content to keep in the shadow of her actress daughter. Gloria, who married twice, once to an American actor and once to a British yachtsman (both marriages ending in divorce) had homes in London and Los Angeles and made sure that she saw her mother as often as possible. She had also kept in occasional touch with her father when living in the same city – New York, where he died before she achieved fame. In 2005, Estelle and Gloria went on holiday together to Montego Bay, Jamaica. On the third evening, when enjoying a 'glorious' dinner, accompanied by champagne, on the terrace of their hotel, Estelle told her daughter: 'This is the happiest moment of my life.' The next morning, having found Estelle face down, perfectly still, with her limbs spread out across her bed as though she was diving into the sea, Gloria told reporters from the Jamaican, British and American press: 'She was a picture of serenity.' At Estelle's funeral in London, a recording was played of her singing 'Just One of Those Things'.

HARRY 'FANCY GOODS' MILLER's relationship with Vera Coleman finally ended and she sold her shoe shop and used the proceeds to pay for her husband, Trevor – who had developed dementia – to have twenty-four-hour, round-the-clock nursing care. She rarely left their home, but devoted herself to his welfare for almost every day of the last three years of his life. Meanwhile, Harry concentrated almost exclusively on his business and successfully made the transition from selling trinkets, souvenirs and cheap brooches and bracelets from a barrow in Brixton Market to taking the lease on a shop within Excelsior Arcade, where he upgraded to exclusive middle-range designer and artisan jewellery. His wife Celia was hospitalised with kidney problems in 1989 and from her hospital bed forgave Harry for his lengthy liaison with Vera, explaining: 'What else could I do? After all, I never told you about my affair with Tom Wistick, the director of my drama group.'

JEFF CALLOWAY (aka Joseph Campbell) bought a house in Cork, in the south-west of Ireland, where he met a Jamaican dance instructor at a yoga class. A month later, she moved in with him. Three months after that, they went back to live in Jamaica.

JOSEPH PELOVSKY ('Spanish Joe'), having received his payout for the Farringdon Road job and without giving any indication, took off to Australia to see his partner Ralph Landau and, much to Benny Pomeranski's chagrin, spent a year there with Ralph between 1954 and 1955 at the end of Ralph's tour with a variety theatre company. In Melbourne, the pair met a fashion designer eager to set up a clothing manufacturing business. 'We are two ducks in water,' Joe wrote to Benny. Within two years, he and Ralph, in partnership with the entrepreneurial designer, had built up a thriving international business introducing the new fashion brand: 'Hispanic'. Later, they extended their operations in the UK and the USA and, at the beginning of the twenty-first century, took up residence in London. Hearing that Bertha Pomeranski was in the process of selling the family business, they made her a better offer than the one she was about to accept and, at the same time, bought the shops on either side of Pomeranski Gowns to create a larger store, where they introduced a new range of male and female leisure and sportswear under the brand 'Hispanic Sports'. They retained the Pomeranski name for the Brixton store, but without the 'Gowns'.

JOYCE GOLUB met a philanthropist from New Zealand at a fundraising meeting for the Valley Ridge Nursing Home, married him after three months and went with him to live in New Zealand.

MAX BASKIN ('Maxie the Ganoff') became so devoted to village life that he took part in local activities, such as the annual fair on the village green. He bought a book a week from a bookshop in Canterbury, taking advice on what to purchase from both the bookshop manager and Benny Pomeranski right up to Benny's last illness. At first, Maxie read only crime fiction (but never even thought of committing any crime himself) but he gradually broadened his horizons. He read *The Secret Agent*, by Joseph Conrad (originally recommended by Benny), three times over one year. He drank beer at the local pub and took a brisk walk every day in all weathers. He bought a dog – a black Labrador – and made friends among his neighbours, only going back to London for Benny's funeral. The woman living in the next-door cottage, a widow, took a strong interest in Maxie's welfare, cooking him meals and introducing him to gardening. They had a quiet register-office wedding in 2001 and died within three months of each other in 2015. He was ninety-six and she was ninety-three.

RONNIE LEWIS married his girlfriend, Hazel, who gave birth to three boys, all of whom grew up bilingually in Spain. For the birth of his first son, named Jeffrey, he threw a big party at the Jax club, to which he invited Bertha, Simon and Marina Pomeranski, Joyce Golub, Jeffrey Calloway and his girlfriend Zena, and Eddie Lawrence and his wife Katrina. 'Big Bill' Crowe was not invited. Ronnie visited London every month to see his mother and sister and to have a meeting with the manager of Lewis and Son, his furniture business in Brixton.

SIMON POMERANSKI cut down his teaching hours at The Blackheath School of Drama to concentrate on writing and directing. His adaptation of *Treasure Island* is still occasionally revived. He has collaborated with his wife Marina on a number of stage productions. Marina also continued to have a successful television career. Their two sons Will and Jonathan took a great interest in their parents' work and Jonathan became and still is an actor. Recently, Simon has taken to writing fiction. His latest novel, written under a pseudonym and closely based on his own family's experiences, is a tale of love, life and death, integrating music, the stage, the fashion business, boxing and crime. It is set in South London, principally Brixton, during the mid-twentieth century.

Acknowledgements

This book was to a significant extent forged in the creative atmosphere of two locations, Cambridge and Soho. In the former, I was able to accelerate and build a momentum for my writing in peaceful college rooms within auras both ancient and modern. The latter, Soho, is the home of my publishers, Quartet, where, in endearingly unvarnished offices, the ancient and the modern also come together. Beyond the university, Cambridge is the home of Anne Garvey, who read my constantly altered and 'honed' manuscripts with great patience and encouragement, and where she and her husband Stephen Brown kept me nourished both mentally and – through Stephen's magnificent cooking – bodily. Fellow guests, friends and facilitators also augmented Cambridge's stimulating atmosphere and I am indebted here to Simon Baron-Cohen, Karina Prasad, Sudesh Prasad, Aaron Kachuck and others. While, back in Soho, my meticulous and ever supportive and sensible editor Peter Jacobs (no relation) kept me grounded and on course throughout. Having now written two novels for Quartet, I do feel I am in good hands including those of guiding individuals above and behind the shop floor, such as David Elliott and, of course, the cultural bastion at the summit, Naim Attallah. Finally, I must acknowledge the influence not of a person but that of a place, the place where I grew up and where much of Pomeranski is set – the dynamic urban village called Brixton.

www.ingramcontent.com/pod-product-compliance
Lightning Source LLC
Chambersburg PA
CBHW011314080526
44587CB00023B/3994